COMPLEMENTARITY

Hugo Daphnis

COMPLEMENTARITY

Translated by Samantha King

AN ESSAY

TITAN-ATLANTE

ISBN 2-9517961-3-7

for Steeve

THE REVELATION

"Do you know what happened to me on the way to work this morning?"

"No, what?"

"Well, I was getting off the tube and heading for my connection as usual. The station was packed and I was lost in thought. The noise was deafening and I was just following the crowd."

"A Monday morning…"

"When suddenly everything around me grew dark and a silence interrupted my train of thought. It was as if everything froze in a deafening silence. The people around me were nothing but mute figures, interrupted in mid flow. I was alone in the middle of all these shapes, which seemed to be stuck in treacle."

"What do you have for breakfast?"

"Stop it, I'm serious! The silence was so shocking I thought I'd turned deaf and then it happened…"

"What are you on about?"

"He arrived! First of all there was a vague shape, hard to make out, and then some details came into focus, like his hand on my shoulder. I stopped breathing as I looked at him. I couldn't tell whether he was looking at me because his face was so bright and contrasted so sharply with the darkness all around. All I could see was a radiance hovering over a diaphanous trail. That's when he spoke to me."

"You saw an angel?"

"And he spoke to me. He said: 'There is only one Consciousness. There is simply only one Consciousness.' I was captivated by his voice – it was so calm and charismatic. It was as if the voice came from within me, and it was telling me something I already knew. I got a glimpse of a beautiful face and then he was gone."

"He flew away?"

"And then everything started moving again – slowly at first and then as fast as ever at rush hour. But I just stood there, motionless, for a second until someone bumped into me and brought me back to reality. I was lost. But I knew I had glimpsed something extraordinary and I haven't stopped thinking about it all day. 'There is only one Consciousness. There is simply only one Consciousness.' Simply…"

"You must have been dreaming. It was just your imagination. You must have nodded off as you were walking."

"Well it seemed real enough any way. And those few words are still ringing in my ears. I'm still all shaken up. You know my eyes watered. I got this feeling of intense detachment – as if I was different from all these people. As if I was a different being."

"Crazy things are always happening to you!"

"Listen, please. You're the first person I've spoken to about it. It wasn't a hallucination or a dream. It was so real. I saw him, I heard him. It was wonderful and terrifying at the same time."

"The way you described him to me, your angel doesn't seem particularly terrifying."

"What scared me at the time, more than this unlikely encounter, was the state of consciousness I found myself in afterwards."

"What do you mean?"

"I felt myself to be terribly alone; as if I had just opened the door into a huge, empty room. I felt alone and frighteningly different from those around me."

"But you have always been different. You're unique."

"Yes I know that. But it really reinforced this persistent feeling I have that I come from another planet; that I'm a stranger on Earth. A little bit like the Little Prince, you know? Like I landed in the middle of a desert one morning and have been wandering in search of a hypothetical return home ever since."

"The Little Prince wanted to go back to his little planet because, after visiting several others, he felt disappointed and let down. That's not where you're at yet. You still have so much to do here on Earth before you go back to where you came from. And even still, I don't think the Little Prince is a good example to follow."

"Why not?"

"Don't you remember what he did to get back to his planet?"

"He found a snake didn't he?"

"He committed suicide."

"OK, it's a little too soon for that. But he saw things differently because he used death as a means of travel. And as a way of never growing old and having to witness the irreversible withering of his body. He will always be of an age where innocence and naivety make him an adventurer who is curious about everything. His heart will be set on exploring his environment, on meeting fellow beings who live differently to each other, on trying to understand them without prejudgements, without tradition and without heritage."

"He formed his own opinion of the world but he didn't like what he saw. That's why he refused to grow up there. But that's not like you is it? Don't tell me you can't see any reason for living in this world. Everything is organised here to enable you to forget about your primary needs so you can devote yourself to much higher tasks. That ought to make you happy surely?"

"At the beginning it did of course. But after studying nature for so long, you come to hope for a real shake-up in it. These daily routines and this infinite repetition of increasingly similar cycles terrify me."

"Mankind now controls nature and mankind's reasoning now dominates Earth."

"But mankind is nature! What is more natural on Earth than man? What arrogance to think we are above nature! Man is fundamentally embedded in the crust of his little planet. His vague yearning towards intergalactic migration will in no way change his status as a natural being."

"The Little Prince grasped that idea pretty quickly. And yet an angel confided in you a truth that ought to change your feelings. It's paradoxical but I believe we should be inspired by the past while maintaining our original innocence in order to live naturally on Earth with other beings. Mankind absolutely has to get a grip so that more children don't refuse to live too."

"I don't follow. What has that got to do with anything? The Little Prince is a fairytale. The angel is an illusion. I'm lost."

DISTORTED ANGEL

I have a firm belief. What I mean is that I too had a revelation. At a certain point in my thinking, an idea induced by the expert application of geometric chaos in a complex process of my consciousness transformed my inner train of thought. It seemed to me at the time that everything fell into place in a complex but clear montage; a simple, wonderful and exciting system.

I am going to tell you honestly about this firm belief. But the complex process that led to such an organisation of my thoughts remains clouded by the obscure effects of my entire history and culture. I cannot, therefore, either express it simply, or prove through an explanation of its internal workings, all the manifest but convincing subtlety of its definition. This is not my aim. So I ask you, if not to trust me then at least to be tolerant in the face of new concepts shown so far.

This is what an angel revealed to me.

There is only one Consciousness. This entity is, of course, void of psychic affiliation to any kind of mortal opportunism. It is unique and shared. In each of us, microscopic individuals who become aware in this middle of the infinite universe, it insinuates itself in our behaviour and transforms our psyche. All humans are aware of this and no doubt a few animals ahead of their genealogical curve have received a fragment of this total Consciousness.

Now that sets the stage for a reasonably exciting adventure don't you think?

Is this not a ground-breaking system for a daring adventurer, disappointed by his latest discovery? Obviously I too aspire to happiness here below. And it would be too cruel of me to have to inform everyone of the evident worthlessness of values, of all values. Especially since that would be the epitome of abjection for my soul wouldn't it?

So I too weave the threads still fresh from an all-too-complex reality to be void of a certain sense of humour. I still laugh about it – a laugh that is a pretext for great cultural strides and more if there is affinity.

But I digress.

So, here we have all these Consciousnesses linked to each other through a shared root. More than that, they form a single entity, shared out among each one of us who finds themselves living amid a tumult of matter. If this is the case, then a great many things are now teetering dangerously on the brink, about to collapse noisily into a monstrously deep gulf.

If I have properly understood what my tortured spirit is trying to say via these lines of obscure and pretentious writing, individuals are but temporal shells of an extract of this 'thing', until the moment when biological functions cease and it returns to the extraordinary maelstrom to be sent on to new adventurers.

THERE IS ONLY ONE CONSCIOUSNESS

"I am sure of it now. The angel revealed the truth to me. Obviously there is only one Consciousness. Obviously it is eternal. Obviously it is the thing all human beings share. From the moment they first gain awareness as a child, they have access to this Consciousness as to a shared treasure. If only they accept the obvious fact. They are but one entity on the surface of this dusty star they occupy so ably."

"We're all brothers – so what?"

"We're more than brothers. The substance that keeps us going – or most of us anyway – is unique. It's about humanity, not humans. And of course death is not an ending or even a departure to a dream place…"

"Heaven!"

"… But a redistribution of this knowledge among all conscious beings. Not only do we have access to all active Consciousnesses but also to the entire history of humanity!"

"You mean to say that from the first time we become aware we are connected with all of humanity, past as well as present?"

"By gaining awareness at about the age of seven, a minuscule fragment of this global Consciousness enters our cerebral cortex and stays with us until we die. Then it returns to the whole before being redistributed again."

"But when we die, this fragment of Consciousness that leaves our mortal coil, does it then find itself in one single child somewhere on Earth?"

"It's important to understand that this fragment of Consciousness that leaves the dying body never left the very definition of the global Consciousness. To put it another way, even if the life story of a man moulds his fragment of Consciousness during his life, his death only means this personal history is dissolved into the Consciousness of humanity. And even though a child might find himself with an historic imprint and the memories of one single deceased person, it's very rare. Usually, the incidences of Consciousness are dissolved into the whole before being reincarnated once more."

"But some lumps might slip through."

"There might indeed be memories of past lives. And why not?"

"It's strange. It's an innovative idea, but I feel like I knew it all along – as if this idea was in each of us, but was hidden by a veil. And even now…"

"The veil of illusions…"

"I think that religions are partly responsible for this lack of visibility."

"What do you mean?"

"I think that religions were written and created in darker times. And this ignorance of reality has remained set in stone, or to be more precise in books. And that hinders the openness of spirit needed to recognise this reality doesn't it?"

"I agree. But don't you think the time has come where anything's possible. I mean religions have shown their limitations. People are asking questions the religions can't answer honestly. Maybe it's time to put forward something else."

"Like what?"

"Well, since you said *you* were visited by an angel, it's quite likely that you're not the only one. Other people might have had the same experience. You all need to start a new movement..."

"That's a great idea but it's going to be a funny old adventure. I think we should start by defining all that comes from this revelation. We have to describe reality using this new frame of reference."

"I'm listening."

"Well, since there is only one Consciousness and it is eternal, at least on humanity's scale, our Consciousness doesn't disappear with death but rather lives again in other bodies."

"For generations and generations."

"So therefore within each of us, as well as the memory of past generations, there is a concrete involvement in them. We all lived through those generations in other forms."

"But the number of Consciousnesses on Earth is going through the roof!"

"And that's the reason for the prevailing unease. The fragment of total Consciousness in each of us is getting smaller and smaller. We feel as if we are being diluted by the multiplicity of occurrences of these receptacles of Consciousness - man. And we look to connect to others because we are looking for ourselves. We need to be close to people, to connect even intimately with people, to recover a little importance in the eyes of the other fragments of Consciousness. That's what associations are about. That's the reason for pooling ideas and feelings. It's why couples form. It's a bit like as if this union offered us an overall view of the totality and filled us with a flawless, and therefore complete, happiness."

"Coming together to compensate for the dispersal of the Consciousness."

"Yes, that's about it."

"The Internet and social networking confirm this idea. Through them we seek to link our feelings and recuperate a supra-entity which offers total awareness. All those connected act together like neurons of the same giant cerebral cortex. And the total Consciousness reappears!"

"And mankind sticks the pieces, the fragments, of this broken sphere – the Consciousness – back together."

"But tell me, if in reality you and I are brothers of some sort, twins who share a part of this global Consciousness, why don't we have access to this total library of memories and feelings, of humanity?"

"But some of us do. Take a look at artists who seem to create beauty out of virtually nothing; in fact they have searched the total Consciousness for ideas to brighten their reality with innovative concepts."

"Inspiration from the muses!"

"Exactly. When an artist composes, writes or paints, he manages to disregard his condition as a fragment of Consciousness encased in this mass of flesh, by temporarily integrating what some would call the perfect World of Ideas, but which is, in fact, nothing other that this interconnection with everything, with the totality, with the total Being or Consciousness …"

"You mean that besides the spirits that agitate inside our skulls, this globality of Consciousness, this total Consciousness also includes matter?"

"But matter as we perceive it is only an idea. We don't have any direct contact with it, only feelings, mathematical calculations or the efforts of our imagination, of our Consciousness. And the reality that surrounds us is but the fruit of our awareness of the world. That's why there can be no rupture between a feeling and the state of the matter which surrounds the nervous system of which it is the subject. To sum up, this total Consciousness includes everything that is, as if on a timeline."

"A timeline of time that doesn't pass any more – a perfect vision of the totality of the Being?"

"Yes, that's right. All feelings treated by fragments of Consciousness, incarnated temporarily in the multitude of conscious beings on Earth since the beginning of this awareness."

"Is that not what some people call God?"

"You can give it a name if you want to but this totality is everyone's identity. We are the holders of a fragment of the perfect, united whole that rings out in our brains and encourages us, day after day, to seek out the fragment that is the Complementarity of our own."

"Like a puzzle?"

"Like a game of building blocks in which we're all supposed to join together to recreate a majestic object that was broken up and the pieces scattered among all our Consciousnesses. And to do so we need to recognise our place within this majestic whole so that we can assume it with due serenity and conviction as we become aware of our role in the temporal movement of humanity, Earth and the universe."

"What next?!"

BEING AN INDIVIDUAL WITHIN A UNITED GROUP

"You know when he spoke to me this morning, I wasn't afraid."

"I know."

"I'm still overwhelmed but I was never afraid. Because I think I had been expecting this for a long time."

"What do you mean?"

"I've always known that each of us has a place in the universe – a place and a reason for being. Once you have found out what it is you can sit back and enjoy it. You have reached the crux of the matter."

"Which is?"

"Happiness of course!"

"Isn't the purpose of life to find our rightful place and never leave it then?"

"To find that place and act in Complementarity with other people and even the whole universe – that's where true happiness lies. I think once you have understood that, you cannot but try to apply it to your whole life. And the obstacles that rise up before you are only the obstacles of a great game. You can even find them exciting when you live free from the trappings of seriousness and solemnity."

"Life is a game."

"And the aim of the game is to be happy."

"From now on, mankind should prepare this path towards incredible happiness. People must unite again and work out possible ways of achieving happiness."

"And that's the role of politics."

"That's right. The role of all politics should be to facilitate conscious action to achieve this goal: to find one's rightful place in the community of mankind and to accomplish this by being themselves."

"And that's when we achieve happiness!"

"Exactly. We just need to be individuals within united groups to be happy. And to do that, we have to find our particular spot, a place where we are totally comfortable, a space to claim and defend."

"To act in Complementarity with the rest of humanity – that's true happiness!"

ACCORDING TO REALITY

According to reality, i.e. the trivial, banal nature of the human condition compared to other scales, politics should be a science capable of harmoniously reconciling the two impetuses that reveal this obvious fact: the involvement of the individual, at the centre of two variations of his own conception (evaluation) of the human being.

Also, from now on the affirmation of an individual identity within a united community should be encouraged by said politics.

Thus the undulatory and corspuscular (tribal and divisional) nature of each thing identifiable in the human being will be hoisted to the pinnacle of the effects of his Consciousness, so that he can finally find satisfaction in the intrinsic (more than intrinsic!) dynamics of the creation of a tangible happiness.

"You know, I'm happy that that angel chose me to relay his truth, the truth. I have always been searching for my place in the community, and this experience has revealed my destiny to me. I finally understand the reason why I'm here: to relay a message."

"You prophet!"

"You may laugh but from now on I'm on a mission. I feel indebted, useful. I'm proud of being where I should be. I'm crying."

"It couldn't have been any other way."

"What do you mean?"

"Only you could be there, in that place, at that moment, on that day. Everything that came before you in time came together so as to produce this wonderful moment. All your successes, but also your failures, contributed to creating the space so that this morning you walked purposefully through the unexpected meanderings of your thoughts and the packed labyrinth of the Paris underground. Your entire life prepared you for this moment blessed by the gods."

"So I shouldn't regret anything?"

"That is literally forbidden to you."

"It's also forbidden to criticise me for the choices that have peppered my chaotic path through life."

"Of course. You have always acted in perfect harmony with a goal you knew nothing of until this morning: preparing for a revelation. How could one criticise you in all honesty? Unless the intention is to hurt you. That's all criticism is good for at the end of the day – introducing fault into another's spirit when nothing justifies that unlikely event. There is no fault when the end result is happiness. Everything is justified in the end!"

"No regrets and no criticism! I like that. Mistakes are worth just as much as successes. They too serve to prepare for the coming happiness. We can take action confidently. No one will be able to criticise us, and we won't be able to regret it. Because if happiness doesn't make the effort worthwhile then death will bring everything back into play again."

"Do you feel calmer now?"

"Of course!"

"Why don't I remember my past lives in other bodies and in other places and times?"

"Some people can."

"But they're fairground attractions! What I mean is why isn't it simpler? It would be really useful if, instead of spending your childhood learning the basics, you were born with that knowledge, if you could open the floodgates to absolute knowledge."

"And know everything about everything!"

"And know everything about the inner workings of the universe."

"Would that make you happier?"

"It would make me more aware!"

"What period in your life have you enjoyed most so far? A period when you lived simply to discover new things. When you lived life to the full without hesitating. When you were filled with happiness simple because it was all new to you. You just had to draw on the momentum that motivated you. With nothing to compare things to, you drew up your own method of interpreting every gesture, every look and every game."

"You mean to say innocence is the greatest gift given to a newborn?"

"It is a precious gift indeed and it is quickly corrupted."

"But why do we choose to destroy it through training ourselves to learn things so damaging to our innate naivety?"

"Because we're afraid of dying."

"What if we re-learnt how to die – the only thing you can be sure of in life. Then we would accept only acquiring knowledge through this deep connection between our bodies and the universe. Knowledge of the universe through knowledge of the self and vice-versa."

"In any case, learning is a game. What's important is that we accept out reintegration into the fabulous maelstrom before we reintegrate younger and more naive bodies. Dying should be a joy: enabling the Consciousness to redraw itself more in harmony with the era, scattering its fragments in young shoots of the human kind, with the secret hope of coming across other Consciousness friends again."

"But my life is nothing but inaction. Before this morning, I had no idea there could be a purpose to all this. I'm never happy except for a few all too brief moments. I prolong my existence searching for these instants that are too rare and too short until I wonder if I'm capable of being happy."

"We have known for a long time that happiness is a dynamic. We can only appreciate this divine instant after having foundered in the dark depths of human sensitivity.

That can be inaction. But it remains an obstacle to our well-being."

"You mean we can't be happy until we have first been unhappy?"

"That's right. But I would go even further. I'm convinced that these two sides of the same coin are shared more equally than anything else among people on Earth - among all beings capable of sensitivity even. We are, in equal parts, subject to the vagaries of an impromptu encounter with our sensitivity, our working nervous systems, and our stimuli and all are capable of creating happiness or sadness. And taking that further, I would say these moments of awareness are filled with joy or sorrow in exactly equal numbers at any given moment on Earth!"

"I really want to believe you because from now on I can call you 'the Visionary'. But this is beyond comprehension. You mean every second on Earth there are as many sad people as happy ones?"

"Yes, that's about it."

"And during our lives we will know joy and sorrow in equal measure?"

"You've got it."

"I find it hard to believe that a young untouchable in Mumbai can be as happy as the son of a Qatari Emir."

"And yet which of them has a big grin on his face any time of the day? One knows simple joys and simple sorrows, while the other experiences infinitely more complex problems. But both of them, deep in their grey matter, have a Consciousness clouded by the release of neuro-transmitters alternating between pleasure and grief. Their surroundings are irrelevant. They are both just as enslaved by their own chemistry. They are both subject to happiness as well as the sorrow that is always with them."

"And what do you mean when you say these two feelings are shared in equal measure at any moment in time on Earth?"

"It's the balance of sensitivities, there is only one Consciousness, and the biosphere seeks balance. And humans seek relief. But in this wonderful world, when a man knows the happiness of being with the person he loves, somewhere else, someone else is going through the awful pain of separation. We have to learn to accept this state of affairs. And as the saying goes: 'The wheel turns.'"

"Each dog shall have his day."

"But just as we learn as much from our mistakes as from our successes, we should learn to see in our sorrow the foundations being laid for a future happiness of equal measure."

"That's great! That should reassure a fair few people."

"We are all equal in the eyes of happiness. We need to learn to be satisfied with it, or to disappear in order to reappear. It's all a game."

"It probably is all a game as you say but it's a cruel one. Some suggest opting out to go somewhere where they're more likely to find happiness. But that's an illusion. Because in order to be activated, joy has to be preceded by sorrow, otherwise it doesn't count! So how can you imagine such a childish concept being challenged? It's nothing but pure invention!

"But necessary to our survival though."

"On the contrary! Can't you content yourself with the melodious juxtaposition of neuro-transmitter releases alternating between pleasure and pain, laughter and suffering…?"

"But it's only momentary. Why this deluge of chemistry?"

"To encourage people to live."

"But what's the big picture? I can only assume that there must be an ultimate goal to all this fine-tuning of such a complicated process. Otherwise it's all just a masquerade, a great game while awaiting the inevitable; the result of a divine, geometric chaos which has got so out of hand it's now uncontrollable."

"Why are you getting so worked up?"

"I'm not worked up. I am just passing on intrinsic grievances to a conscious humanity. It's all fine having found and recognised God in the sum of Consciousnesses, but if it's to abandon him to the role of a child learning the complexities of a game of deduction, then it is absolutely lamentable!"

"Do you consciously concern yourself with one particular cell in your body? No! You decide on the general direction of the whole, of your entire body, so calm down."

"I'll calm down when you have brought me proof of an objective reason for my presence here on Earth!"

WE WILL ALL HAVE A SECOND CHANCE

Life is a game.

And the ultimate aim of the player is to do the best he can with the elements at his disposal at the outset. We still have to define what "the best he can" means. We imagine it is a hazy concept, bathed in altruism and citizenship. And if we fail to construct a lawful and happy existence, and we unexpectedly draw the 'go straight to jail' card, it is highly likely we would launch a staunch defence of that extremely modern concept that is the death penalty. Why? So we could start all over again…

Because it is now clear that the unified nature at the heart of the substance shared among all Consciousnesses cannot be diminished. And if the number of people continues to increase, the share of this whole will be greatly reduced in each one of us. That is why it is so necessary to join forces around an idea for example. In the end, death will put an end to the active state of this fragment of the whole and set in motion a new arrangement of miniscule fragments. That is the simple finality of this global momentum. But as we have seen, living souls do group together and the whole becomes palpable again.

So death is just a detail in this fabulous arrangement, a laughable fraction of time.

To find yourself at the age of first awareness, in possession of this fragment of this imperious sphere is both a great responsibility and an amusing masquerade. In fact it is more than likely that in the coming years the incidence of a being on the universe will be nothing more than a conceit. Then we will begin to learn how to defer to the laws drawn up by other Consciousnesses in other times, that is to say by a different arrangement of our common origin, like following the rules of a great communal game. And the insignificant part of the whole will discover his junk ego and at last join in the game.

It is time now to stop this excess revealed in the lingering scent of sorrow equally shared with the joy we chase after. All that is nothing but a masquerade. And it is better to smile behind a mask…

Because we will have a whole other life to rival Sisyphus.

A SHARED DIVINITY

"You would like to be able to identify with this global Consciousness. You wish that it, like you, was subject to the whims of the chemistry in your brain. You would like it to bend to the geometric chaos that rules your character. But don't fool yourself; it is of a different order."

"This god doesn't amuse me."

"Well obviously. He couldn't care less about your amusement. He is a being that oversees space and time. He is perfect and therefore of absolute beauty. That explains why those who are capable of obtaining direct access to him, to explore fully their art, are great creators of beauty. They reproduce perfect and carnal forms, inspired by their connection with the perfect World of Ideas. Isn't that the fairest way of bringing about ecstasy and ecstatic happiness?"

"Of course. But what you are suggesting here lays the foundations of a much too innovative religion, and makes inspired artists the clergy of your church!"

"Let's be clear, I'm not suggesting anything. We're just trying, remember, starting with this revelation, to deduct a new frame of reference for interpreting reality. So far I have only put forward hypotheses so that we can test them against our experience of reality. But the artist as a proactive force for an unlimited access to happiness – now there's an idea!"

"Which renders null and void all the emasculating efforts of official religions."

"It would be like a new human ethic which dared at last to restore religion's primary meaning: bringing people together rather than dividing them."

"Complementarity as apposed to communities."

"That's it exactly."

SLENDER

I still have a hope, albeit a slender one, that all this has meaning. It would be a real shame if the pessimists were right. And yet all indications point to the irreversible ascendancy of divine geometric chaos. So, evidently the instigation of this jumble of cause and effect was a divine stimulus. But this fortunate divinity isn't in the slightest bit a regrettable creation. He doesn't care, nor does he care about the personification that we saddle him with. We got that wrong!

So there is, like an innate violent anger, a momentum that pushes us to improve ourselves. But this last trace of divinity within us is only there to increase time and a lasting time at that.

That is what reassures me about it. I limit myself to existing for me and a few others who are dear to my heart. But the awful disappointment I find down here terrifies me. It is enough to make you ask questions isn't it?

But eternal renewal appeals to me. I would like to be born again over time, unexpectedly transposed into the Consciousness shared by some people, living in different eras, seeking to conquer once more the late-lamented unity through association or through love, joining the great inter-human movements; there you have the great weakness in this lowly lump of meat.

Imagine for a moment a world populated by a limited number of brave young people. The grief created by us having such small fragments of the broken whole would be greatly alleviated. The total Consciousness would find the stagnant reservoirs that are the elderly, filtered out. And life would be able to re-deploy all its art and pleasure-seeking comfort to create happiness. That's one win!

The last snippets of Consciousness traumatised by age would have been moved on to brand new bodies. And the rarer fragments would find themselves boosted by a welcome vigour.

There would be everything to gain from abandoning old bodies and rejoining the magnificent age of the first years of joy.

Let's stop cursing the passing of time. Instead of watching lives which follow on one after the other and deaths which signal the failure of molecules, let us rejoice at dying so we can be born again here on Earth, sharing with as many young children as life has managed to create to play.

Dying is the most beautiful thing life can offer us: the power to play at innocence once more.

"But tell me, aware beings form one single entity. This fragmented Consciousness that is present in billions of minds only has one goal: to come back together. All these Consciousnesses, when they leave the bodies they have inhabited, are sent out again to youngsters and even other Consciousnesses why not? So the members of a community have every chance, when they die, of creating a blue streak in the spirit of the ungodly in the eyes of this assembly of souls."

"You mean that in the next generation they risk finding themselves in the body of those they despised in the last?"

"Obviously! It's one of the ingredients of the great game these actors devote themselves to. But admit it; it's a bit ridiculous isn't it?"

"I admit."

"A whole life to build up your dream of absolute happiness just to, like everyone else, start over and over again. Well this is a strange problem. If our ultimate goal is to reconstitute our roots, glue back together the pieces of this broken sphere, while everything combines to scatter the pieces far and wide again, where are we going?"

"I don't understand. I thought it was clear. Internet and social networks recreate the virtual neurons where the scattered colours of a new incarnation of the Consciousness are covertly born. There is our goal! Once we have reactivated the premises of a divine momentum, once each of us has found their place and is working to strengthen it in Complementarity with humanity, we will have achieved our ultimate goal."

"And we'll die again."

COMMUTATIVE EXACTION

In a prophetic dream, somewhere beyond the clouds, I carefully construct the various paths that will enable me to find the inspiration I need to create the structure of my new life. I consider this food because it is essential to my psychic balance. I don't want to deteriorate, at least not yet.

Of course I am alone, and will be for some time yet. I do not yet know what the divine geometric chaos has in store to lift my life to a commutative level of clear contours! I am getting a little carried away again. But I want today more than ever. I want these contours to agitate each cell of my body like a rattle. In every instant of my short existence I want there to be emotions, I want the most unsettling emotions to assail me like an assault on a poorly defended fortress...

Tonight again I content myself with persevering in this being that still amazes me. How can you not laugh at this pile of blood that frolics more than it realises? I should make a king or a philosophy of it but I calmly apply myself to making a mad man, a winged mad man but a mad man all the same.

So of course I am going to react. I am going to destroy all the obstacles and build an aura of fire. After the smoky agonies of literature, after the illustrious sounds of harmonious mechanics, I am going to throw myself body and soul into the activity of the third millennium: commutative exaction.

The lyrical offering of a whole generation, this is the lair of a majestic tradition of gold diggers. It is the bare truth. It is the particularity of any slightly honest life. It is the work of a god, the exaction of princes!

And if I apply to this abstract idea the all too evident mechanics of commutativity, it is because I have faith in my madness. I believe it is what will lead me to the summit of assumed concepts. I believe in my reactivity faced with the offending recurrences of low, alimentary thoughts. But after that I will need to rest…

It is clear; I don't come from this planet.

"You know something?"

"What?"

"I can't wait for him to come back. I have tons of questions to ask him. It's easy to slip such a truth into the spirit of the weakest, but I'm not going to be pushed around!"

"What are you talking about?"

"Well after all that, after all this high-level, intellectual shilly-shallying, I still haven't got anywhere."

"All the same, you have contributed to the production of a universal philosophy capable of bringing happiness and serenity…"

"We did say that in order for happiness to exist, it must be accompanied by sadness in the same measure. So I don't think the philosophy will catch on very quickly."

"But it was told to you by an angel!"

"He only revealed the enigmatic prologue. It's a little facile to deliver such a truth to a being in search of the absolute. Of course I am happy to have been chosen. But wouldn't it have been simpler to just insert this truth in the spirit of children from birth? That way everyone would start their lives with the same foundation."

"And isn't that the case?"

"If it was the case then why was this simple truth – 'there is only one Consciousness' – communicated so flippantly, with such room for error? Altruism, for example, which slipped in to the foundation of all human communities - into *the* human community even - is just a rough outline of the consequences of the supreme revelation. Connecting with others, compassion, helping each other – these are just signs of a frantic search to incorporate the values laid down in these five words. We have all pretended to ignore such a simple reality. But now it is there, stripped of its fanciful attire, pure."

"That implies a total revision of morals!"

"A moral reform, yes."

"Morals finally shared in the understanding of all the occurrences of Consciousness on Earth."

"We are laying here the basis for a new understanding on Earth."

"If I've understood correctly, all aware lives will find themselves united under a shining cupola of the same origin?"

"More than that. Since the reality of this superior Consciousness collects the experiences of all its members over time, it is itself detached from the temporal sequence of events of the Being."

"I don't understand."

"Well, it is removed from time. So it is not the instigator of occurrences of Consciousness, but is the very essence of them, shared in each of us."

"And death has no meaning since this entity is immortal."

"It is just a fortuitous rearrangement, but the essence does not disappear."

"That's what everyone already believes isn't it?"

"Perhaps. But the novelty here is in revealing at last the human nature of god, in that he appears for the juxtaposition and the arrangement of the Consciousnesses and the divine nature of man in that he has, within himself, a fragment of this divinity. And the outward sign of the beginning of the arrangement of these scattered pieces is happiness. To sum up, happiness reveals a step towards the divine."

"From now on, the living don't deserve respect. Life isn't respectable; only happiness is, in that it evokes the partial reconstitution of a larger fragment of the total Consciousness."

"That's about it."

"We should praise happy people because they alone are on the path to a Complementarity suitable for reconstructing the concrete and perfect dynamic for the coherent assembly of all Consciousnesses."

"That's lovely."

EVERYTHING IS FINE!

I have to tell you something. I have to get down to work now and do my best to explain an idea that is rather new, an idea that won me over during my travels in the World of Ideas. It took me a little time to understand it but now I am sure: all this finally explains why I was put here. And that's important to know to give me the strength to break away from the current lethargy that encourages the average person to bury themselves in business and consumerism. Because away from the daily routine of our modern societies, lies a magnificent aura that many, many people find captivating. This wonderful plan that directs the hand of the painter or sculptor, which fills a composer or an author with understanding, which brings clarity to the tortured reasoning of the mathematician, is the same plan that now gives me the strength to challenge ideas approved via a mass of limited demonstrations. And this new concept's originality is but further proof that I am right to devote my time and energy to it here on Earth, right now.

So what is it all about? First man needs to be freed from his illusions and made to face up to his unfortunate position in the Being. Then I would carry out a much-needed reorganisation in which everyone would have their place, a position from which they could defend their individuality within a united group. The ground-breaking principle that governs this divine assembly is called Complementarity. It is what defines the path each individual takes as he finds his place in society. And this place defines the individual as an element of society. And this element can defend his individuality by accepting his defining position in the heart of community mechanics.

QED!

"Joy drives us to accomplish this divine project. So why was that not always the case?"

"Because some people led us astray; we were blinded by the comforts of fringe benefits, blinded by altruism, blinded by communitarianism, blinded by introspection."

"The prophets?"

"They felt something all right. But they thought their ideas were dictated to them by someone else, when in fact they came from within themselves via an opening into the World of Ideas, where all history and feelings are shared. They only saw the effects, without seeing the simple cause."

"There is only one Consciousness?"

"That's right."

"But then all you have done is talk with yourself?"

"From the very beginning…"

REJOINING THE UNITY BEFORE BEING SHARED OUT AGAIN

"So the meaning of life is happiness. Without that, life makes no sense any more. Those unsuited to happiness should be able to choose to rejoin the whole so they can start out again. They can either play again, by rediscovering the joys of the early challenges, or disappear from this manifestation, while being aware of their eternal return."

"You want to make suicide common practice?"

"I want to give all those who have reached the end of their experiment with their life on Earth the chance to re-learn how to die. People have to be able to understand and accept that the round of the game they are playing right now can end, and that they can rejoin the whole before being dispersed once more."

"To join in the next round…"

"And offer everyone the ideas and experiences of their own contact with a world in motion…"

"To bring people closer together in a community of feelings…"

"And encourage them to rejoin the whole..."

"Through happiness…"

MOURNING

What if the hurt that accompanies the loss of a loved one were completely futile?

Don't misunderstand me, I am not denying that it can be painful to be refused access to a certain arrangement of matter. But once you understand that each Consciousness is extracted from a single whole, a sort of supra entity that some like to give a name to they can embrace it more easily, all attempts to personalise heartache become null and void.

To put it another way, as we are all brothers and complementary by essence, as our common goal is the serenity of perfect mechanics, when someone dies, their individuality freed from its earthly shell rejoins the possibilities of being of all the Consciousness effectively in action. The talent is shared. Sometimes chance plays with destiny and a human being is born with a large part of the individuality of someone who has died. But the whole of the innate and, why not, a large part of the acquired which would have migrated towards the unpredictable meanderings of 'the soul', are forever reborn in the billions of active conscious nervous systems.

Isn't that great?

We don't really die. We redistribute ourselves in a different way. We readjust in another optimal configuration.

And all those who gain awareness, just like when you get the creativity bug, only disappear from their apparent forms – wasted and aged – to reappear elsewhere in other forms. A never-ending new beginning, an impromptu but continual rebirth over the millennia that separate us from the first time.

But how do you escape the cycle of rebirth?

"Everything is ephemeral! Feelings, consequences, lives – all disappear so as to reappear in a changed form in the wonderful flow of billions of cycles, offset and intertwined with each other."

"You really are inspired!"

"And yet I'm having trouble shaking off an idea, an idea that shows how enslaved I am to ideas defended by the old religions."

"What is it?"

"It's about the death of people… I am aware that the multiplication of instances of Consciousnesses on Earth due to the demographic explosion slows progress towards the absolute happiness which will result from the reconnection of all Consciousnesses into a single entity. Firstly because it means many, many more connections have to be made. But secondly because it undoubtedly makes the intellectual approach more complex and how do you get the message across to such a large number of people?"

"So we have to slow this demographic expansion."

"Altruism taught as a dogma by certain major religions has only made it harder to take an honest look at the problem. First of all, how do we reduce this outrageous dispersal of ever smaller fragments of the total Consciousness?"

"Perhaps we should restore the power of natural selection, a power lately neutralised by a rise in philanthropy?"

"You mean stop saving lives?"

"I mean accepting the sudden return of some to the whole, before being dispersed again so as to improve the general state of active nervous systems and therefore their ability to flood the World of Ideas with new sensations."

"To rejuvenate the population?"

"That's right. Because an innocent being, with his quest for knowledge and experience, is a much more prolific and effective donor if you measure him by his daily quota of sensations and innovative concepts."

"So we would have to encourage the elderly to accept dying in order to be reborn."

"When you put it like that it can't be too difficult can it?"

"Don't fool yourself. Many hang on until the very last, as long as hope endures."

"But isn't hope increased here?"

"But it's a hope based on your new system. And it has little in common with the traditions that have become dogmas. They would all have to turn their backs on their old value system and sign up unreservedly to this new frame of reference. That's unlikely, among the elderly. They will prefer to hang on to their old traditions because that is what they geared their whole life towards. I don't think your new procedures will receive a warm welcome with them unfortunately."

"So we have to focus on the young, on those not taken with ancestral traditions."

"That would be a better idea. Perhaps once they have been taught, they can convince the older ones."

"Then we have to simplify this enormously. This interpretation must come across as stemming from what is real – as if the veils of illusion raised by religions over centuries were blown away, revealing a simply and obvious truth."

"And that is the truth! I'm still blown away by it."

"Do you feel that excitement that grips mathematicians when they are studying a problem and suddenly it resolves itself in front of their eyes into a solution filled with naivety, simplicity and beauty?"

"It's true that all this is pretty simple in the end. No more need for parables and poetic legends. It can all be summed up in these few words: There is only one Consciousness. There is simply only one Consciousness. The rest is nothing but deduction and commentary. How come we didn't work it out long ago?"

"An angel had to travel."

"He came at the right moment."

"For once…"

REVISION

Listening to the voices that had inspired me, the *bona fide* connections between my soul and the wonderful thread of the absolute Consciousness, I wept like a child. And it wasn't the first time. Just this morning, on comprehending the chance interpretation of the product of one other than myself, I cried.

And even now, tears fill my eyes. It is as if I have an over-riding need to express my helplessness in the face of this influx of well-ordered ideas. I have to apply myself. The task ahead is huge but it must be done.

Let's get back to it.

Earth encloses much more than we might think. There is a diaphanous cloud to which all the occurrences of this newly-revealed Consciousness are attached. There are, then, several levels of perception of this blue entity. The second level requires the carrying out of an in-depth study of the values defended by the supreme creation: man, abstract of course!

This wonderful, offensive, sublime thread, which constantly preserves its strict and rigorous form, its rugged form which boasts of the little faith of its tutors... I am getting a little carried away! Let me present the source of my inspiration, and of all others at the same time, the everlasting source of the most innovative and ground-breaking concept. Here then is the musician's muse and the writer's imagination.

And this fountain which quenches the thirst of its most faithful followers never ceases to reveal through its form the sublime question of sense. Why such a construction? Why did it shatter its metaphoric essence and scatter the fragments among minds ready to receive them. What can we do other than rejoice in this irrefutable fact?

But if by rejoicing, we mean crying day after day then I am crying a river all the way to the ocean!

It is amazing to think that such a process remained hidden until so recently. It is as if artists preferred to cloak the machines of gods. All very enigmatic...

But nowadays I am more of a scientist aren't I?

Those who reserve the right to appear brilliant have something very simple in common: they let themselves be guided by the electrical plan which tells their neurons how to arrange themselves. It is a little like a mother's reassuring hand holding that of her child's, regulating the amount of freedom she allows him within the limits of safety. Or even more like the teacher's lesson which, repeated often enough, shapes the student's morals by example.

There is, therefore, something beyond the boundaries of perception. And each door into this World of Ideas is a connection to the total communication of the understanding of man, of all mankind, even the dead since their understanding will have been absorbed into the whole as part of the redistribution plan. (I am sure I will be understood one day.)

At the end of the day, it is simply the proof that original creations are just on loan from an absolutely perfect creativity. And moreover, shared by all those who put in a bit of effort. Once you accept that, it must be a little difficult to accept awards!

So we have then a river of concepts which irrigates the spirit of the lucky who are able to use this to build their social base – or pervert it like martyrs... And we have these wonderful links which force open the locks more easily than an emergency exit springs open in times of need. As for artists, they are the hostages of such success; they are forced to bail out the excess liquid or risk drowning in it at any moment.

And that is why they cry...

"I think it is time to sum up our thoughts. After such a surprise, it would be normal for your spirit to go into a tail spin reviewing this new conceptual field. But we have to simplify this new data so as to present it in its best light. This discovery is simple, coherent and very beautiful."

"I am aware of that. What do you want to start with?"

"With the first time you become aware of yourself, that fabulous instant that seems to define the entire aura of a future life."

"It's the moment of individualism, when that tiny fragment of total Consciousness bonds with a mind and forgets where it came from. The person this happens to trades their original naivety for an innocence steeped in memory and serenity. This is the time when destiny lays its foundations."

"The child becomes aware of concepts which may put him at odds with his environment."

"Yes. He seems to be inspired by an invisible world. He goes through his senses, searching for replications of that which the World of Ideas inspires in him. This is the period when he seems to plunge into a free creative fervour."

"But it's not free?"

"It cannot be achieved without inspiration at least. And as the young child only has a truncated vision of reality, that inspiration draws on the brand new connections between his body and the total Consciousness. So he finds matter to produce in reality, inspired by all these sensations recorded since the beginning of time. And as if stripped of all taboos, his creativity is all the more unbridled. He will have difficulty later in recovering this magic ability of childhood. If he practices or trains hard enough, or if he is particularly gifted, he may be able to use it. In that case he will join the wonderful caste of artists."

"If I understand you correctly, this young child is more creative than his elders because his spirit hasn't yet been cluttered with secular traditions or preconceptions."

"That's exactly it. His novice understanding offers no obstacle to the majestic flow of divine inspiration. He creates with infinite ease."

"But it won't last."

"Indeed not. The education he will receive will build a barrier between the total Consciousness and his own."

"How?"

"By instilling in him selected and measured concepts. By educating him, his parents and teachers will break the harmonious relationship linking his Consciousness to those of others. He will individualise himself."

"Isn't that a normal process? I mean even alone, roaming humanity, he will substitute an observed experience for divine inspiration."

"It's likely. In any case, the result is that he individualises himself and obstructs the channels that link him to the whole."

"And it is only through training, or affected by the twists and turns of his life, that he will be able to experience this majestic disposition towards creativity once again. He will feel himself inspired by the muses and his fingers will move in infinite ways, guided by a continual flow of ideas…"

"The source of which is in the immense total of past experiences."

"And the compilation of this flow, in the artistic process, goes straight back to this Consciousness of humanity like a new experience that can then inspire others and so on…"

"Such is creation on Earth."

"After which, the child loses his innocence, loses his privileged relationship with Nature, and joins the overpopulated ranks of the human community. From then on, he must find his place. He must be able to establish his individualism in this united group. By occupying a role that enables him to stand out within a fraternal society, he undertakes to make the realistic optimism of Complementarity his own."

"And he is happy!"

"He is serene and happy to be able to display original creativity within the reassuring context of conceptual stability."

"That's happiness! Being able to exist intensely, by standing out from those around you while still finding reassurance from them."

"Being the complement of all others…"

"To enable humanity to progress towards its destiny."

"Because we all have a fragment of the total Consciousness which has temporarily joined our minds and which, upon our death, will return to the whole before being sent out again."

"And perhaps it is during this temporary reunion that the new sensations recorded by the Consciousness in transit are transferred so as to join all those already in store!"

"That makes it sound a little like a trading port."

"Memories of childhood games…"

AN OBVIOUS COMPLEMENTARITY

"Let's go back, if you don't mind, to the search for Complementarity. It's not just about looking for a job, as some would have us think. But above all, it's about being aware of your supposed role within the community of humans. Some will follow their instinct, but I think one of the missions of education, rather than simply cluttering the paths of access to the divine, is to teach students to discover and assume their position in society."

"Why would there only by one possibility?"

"In the absolute that is the case! The aim of the game is just that; to find the place where you can act in Complementarity with everyone else."

"Like the mechanics of a clock?"

"More than that! More than a simple job beneficial to the temporal progress of society (even delinquents have a role to play there); this is about a position in which you find yourself in complete symbiosis with your environment. In other words, it gives us as much in stimulus as we give it in creativity."

"By that you mean everyone is an artist?"

"All children are. And if education hadn't unfortunately blocked their access to the fabulous catalogue of human sensations, they would still be artists as adults. The truth is, it wouldn't take much for some to become artists again."

"A revelation would do it?"

"You've got it."

"A human community made up of budding artists, playing happily while forging their individual personalities and offering the community the result of their efforts in exchange for the protection of the characteristics of their personality – that is the vision of a world where the eulogy of Complementarity is a universally accepted precept."

"What worries me a little, aside from these crazy extrapolations whose more than hypothetical nature you have shared with me, is that for this new interpretation of reality to work, it would have to be accepted by as many people as possible. How do you plan to go about that? Would it be by suggesting a mechanism that disparages all other ideas? How do you want to convince the stubborn?"

"I already told you. While this interpretation seems brand new, the facts it reveals already exist. Altruism really is the foundation of human society. Most people enjoy getting together with others to share the same sensations. People form couples. The search for a partner can be stronger than anything else. Man needs others to fulfil his being and to become who he has actually been from birth. All these facts are already included in the definition of the human being."

"Exactly. Since it is an irrefutable fact, don't you think things work well enough to enable humanity to simply carry on?"

"But the population is exploding. That's a problem not only for the environment but also for people's sense of identity. How do you find your place in a population which is becoming terrifyingly big?"

"And the solution is to see ourselves as brothers or cousins?"

"The solution, indeed, is to recognise the same original inner spark that animates us, this Consciousness that pushes us to ask so many questions. And for two reasons: Firstly to recognise the dispersal of one single entity in all conscious beings, then we will accept more easily the idea of dying to be freed from the worn out carbon compounds that encase us and find newer ones. It is easier to leave the cradle of humanity if we know we will be returning. And secondly because reality presented in this way brings us a little closer together. Bonds are stronger in a fraternity, especially faced with the inevitable obstacles and twists and turns."

"Humanity finds itself rejuvenated."

"More than that, an awareness of the clumsy dispersion of such a jewel among such an enormous number of people will encourage more responsibility when it comes to having children."

"You mean there will be fewer children too?"

"The number of people will stabilise. In order for a child to be born, an old person must give up their place."

"And then the fragment of Consciousness that was in the old person can be reincarnated in the child!"

"It's not quite as straightforward as that. When the child first becomes aware, it will acquire a fragment of the conglomerate formed by all past Consciousnesses. So he will be given an entity stripped of a specific history, just a connection to the memory of the feelings of humanity."

"A connection that is easy and automatic during childhood but that becomes problematic later."

"Indeed only the most talented or adventurous will have the ability to draw almost consciously upon this substance abounding with ideas for the essence of their work."

"The others will be merely spectators."

"Generators, by their sheer number, of a powerful current of confederating sensitivity which, upon their death or even earlier, will rejoin the sum of past sensations."

"And all can start over again in an unchangeable cyclical movement."

GOD IS THE SUM OF ALL CONSCIOUSNESSES

I need to explain myself tonight. This morning, as I was wandering along the corridors crowded with strangers in a Parisian station as usual, an angel came to speak to me. This intangible and hazy angel whispered in my ear something I had known all along: the Consciousness of those who open themselves to the world of ideas is unique. It is a single entity. Some call it God or intuition, some can connect with it easily after a little training and may therefore seem inspired by their muses, some have never yet accessed it and consequently they are rarely men.

This absolute network which links all Consciousnesses who can connect to it is the very basis for a new dynamic: Complementarity.

The revelation of this irrefutable fact explains an awful lot: The inspiration of artists and the great improvisers is an essence shared by all. You just need to go with the flow to interpret generous harmonies in the real world. This established and organised essence, or at least that is how it seems at our level of perception, is the thread that unites us all; an intangible bond which makes us more than similar elements of the same species. It makes us the fragments ripped from the original sphere which divides into ever smaller pieces to keep pace with the number of instances. The more the population increases, the more this share of original Consciousness is reduced in each of us. And a malaise grips the new-comers.

To remedy this, we need to organise associations of individuals who, in the Complementarity they feel in coming together, can recapture a little of the happiness that evaporated as the number of occurrences of fragments of Consciousness increased.

That's it - more or less...

"Since we started this discussion, we have mainly been talking about the aspiring artist who manages to distinguish himself in the advantageous exploitation of a flow of sensations we have chosen to call the total Consciousness and that some others prefer calling the World of Ideas or God. But the majority no longer have access to this profusion of concepts or do not pay attention to it."

"The vast majority in reality."

"It is important to position them too within a society based on the principles of Complementarity."

"I think they have found their place in society. They act in perfect Complementarity with others and so they are happy too, aren't they?"

"In which case, life for them really is a game. But if someone is struck by a serious disease that handicaps them for life, one could imagine that, unable to foresee any future possibility for happiness, they might decide to cut short that life to rejoin the totality of Consciousness before being included in a new redistribution. In short, give themselves the possibility of a new basis for a new life?"

"It certainly is an attractive bet!"

"In the same way, someone who is so unhappy they are in despair, who sees no chance of possible joy, should be able to find in death the possibility of changing their person and era in the great game of life on Earth."

"The game analogy makes perfect sense! Like when you want to start a new game so you reset the score, someone wanting to start life over can choose to die."

"And their Consciousness, after having been reincorporated in the others, will be redistributed in young children of whatever origin, from their first intuitions about the infinite."

"It's clear you would have to be really disappointed with this life to run the risk of finding yourself in an even worse one!"

"Play is an adventure…"

"Within this temptation to seek a happy life, there is an unfathomable despair which could lead to a grandiose and painful end."

"But isn't it preferable to letting yourself die of old age, waiting until the mechanisms in your cells seize up and cause incoherence and chaos within a body that has done its best?"

"At the cost of the happiness of others?"

"What others? We agreed at the start we were indivisible. Isn't leaving by creating as much death as possible a revenge on nature through a gesture likely to moderate the population expansion?"

"But by adding sorrow to those left behind!"

"It's true that for those who have not yet acquired the clairvoyance of this new appreciation, the pain may be infinite. The grief born of a sudden rupture between two nervous systems reveals the unity that each of us seeks to spread. That which we are used to calling love, whether it be family or other, is the proof of a universal momentum bringing together people."

"And animals…"

"Don't race ahead! Pain born of a separation, whether temporary or definitive, is part of the definition of human nature. But progress towards the concept of an eternal return should also bring relief. By identifying the total Consciousness as an entity which oversees the fragments of Consciousness in each of us, by recognising the similar and complementary nature in all of us, we build an unflagging bond between ourselves and others. The loss felt by the definitive departure of a loved one on their death, should be moderated by the persistence of this bond. And the absence of stimulus emitted by this loved one, their effective absence, can be likened to an absence in the window of study of one's own senses."

"You're going too far there!"

"No, listen. When someone dies, they still exist in the memory of those who loved them."

"That doesn't mean they're still there!"

"It simply means that as long as someone is thinking of them, that person exists as much as if they were standing silently behind the person. They cannot be seen or heard, but they maintain their place in that person's Consciousness."

"Which means people are immortal as long as we keep them in our thoughts?"

"Which means death is not a solid concept at all. If we are talking about an arrangement of matter around a fragment of Consciousness whose atoms change function then yes, it can be painful to lose someone. But we know they will reappear in other forms in another place and will endure a while longer on the surface of their own Consciousness."

"Getting back to those who want to kill as many people as possible when they kill themselves, doesn't that make them spoilsports?"

"Obviously it upsets the pattern of play somewhat. And in no way do I seek to inspire kamikazes. But isn't it the last throw of the dice of a spoilt child?"

"You could put it that way."

"Here you have someone who, endowed with this fragment of Consciousness that others are still envious of, has made a big mistake in the aesthetics of life. He is completely unaware of reality and lives as if in a dream…"

"That could be said of many human beings."

"Disappointed and let down, he does not achieve the happiness he hoped for and makes the unfortunate decision of leaving an indelible trace in the memory of his audience. He kills himself taking as many active nervous systems with him as possible."

"In any case, everything will begin again with the next delivery of reasonings awaiting their blue lights…"

"It's a bit like a player who, having not earned enough points to go through to the next round, decides to make the most of the crazy graphics of his games console by committing virtual suicide!"

"But in this case it's not virtual."

"You know, all this bothers me. If we continue on this theme, I feel I'll be capable of justifying the unspeakable. I could ask you what the difference is between virtual and real. You would tell me that in real life, that sort of an action causes a lot of suffering. And I would say that in this reality, all that suffering would be counterbalanced by a happiness just as intense, somewhere on Earth. In the end I would manage to justify, even encourage, such a barbaric act."

"You mean mass murder is good for the biosphere?"

"I mean that if we change the scale of exploration of this reality, everything instantly loses gravity. Nothing matters any more on Earth when you start studying the stars. And the population control vital to the sustainability of our environment cannot be achieved without death, for want of hindering life. So rather than limiting the birth of little ones, who still have an innate faculty for naive adventure and creation and who only recuperate well-travelled fragments of Consciousness a little later, the elderly whose tired and worn bodies have reached the limit of their regenerative possibilities should allow their Consciousnesses to rejoin the World of Ideas before being sent back out to the young who are ready to use all their new strength to conquer the world of the real."

"But from that to exterminating them!"

"This end has to be accepted consciously. Just like the old Native Americans who, seeing that their mission on Earth was drawing to a close, would go into the mountains to die, reason and the knowledge of the cycle of life can encourage worn nervous systems to prove their love and respect for the human species, through agreeing to leave their senile bodily shell."

"So we don't need to exterminate each other?"

"No, indeed it isn't indispensible."

"And once the divine cycles are integrated into everyone's Consciousness, they will no longer need to search for their final destiny. Everyone will simply want to end this phase of the cycle in the best possible way, making newly available for all, via the intervention of the World of Ideas, a collection of sensations, each more extraordinary than the last, thus attesting to the exceptional destiny which has just finished, before stirring up the ballet of concepts leading straight to the notion of reincarnation."

"Before that you have to live though."

"It's vital."

"But what then is the ideal life in your view? Does it have to necessarily be short and manic rather than meditative and calm?"

"I think what is important is that it should be peppered with intense and personal feelings. As his passage on Earth draws to a close, each man should be able to offer other humans a quality compilation of the most touching moments of his existence."

"Whether they be moments of frantic activity or of quiet meditation?"

"Anything that could strengthen the definition of mankind. Anything that will teach him to define himself in this wonderful conceptual exception that is life on Earth."

"So ultimately what's needed is for each and every one of us to express all our individuality in order to receive in return the stimulus necessary for the emergence of intense and memorable sensations. To exist so as to resonate in return!"

"And in order for this individuality to reveal itself to others, in order that its existence can finally have meaning within the excess of individuals, we need to find the ideal activity within the society we live in. An activity which will offer us a means of social expression and meet our material needs to keep us going."

"For artists, the question does not even arise. The ideal activity would be the creation of new concepts dictated by the majestic blend of human sensations via divine inspiration. But what about for the many others, those who have forgotten the winding road which leads to the world of muses and who struggle every day to persevere in their body?"

"Through productive work they will offer up a proportion of their time to the benefit of the community, in exchange for a negotiable power with their peers. Most will work for a private company which will give them a salary in return for their productivity."

"The very existence of these companies then is that: offer an activity in return for a salary. Everything else is secondary."

"From now on it is clear that a company ought to contribute to the happiness of the citizens and the nation where it was founded. It is out of the question that a company should offshore its activity – that makes no sense. Why would you give up the chance to bring joy to your fellow citizens and transfer your main activity thousands of miles away? The first mission of a company is to provide its employees with the means of living a happy life!"

"But if you hold that all humans share the same identity, isn't it contradictory to want to preserve the happiness of some to the detriment of others? Whether the company offers an activity to people here or elsewhere, the result is the same isn't it?"

"What you have to realise is that when humans join forces, it is to recover a little of the power they lost through the dispersal of the fragments of Consciousness. Together they have every reason to fight other groups for their right to happiness. By opposing others they generate sensations, whether they are beneficial or not."

"And that can end in war."

"Yes because the policies instigated to incite equal access to happiness can run contrary to one another. This isn't usually the case. Tensions are easing and rivalry is generally more sporting. But it is within these continuous struggles that are born the dynamics that favour renewed interest in the constancy of reality of the people who comprise them."

"You need a struggle to understand the importance of the game and to enable new sensations to fill your own understanding."

"You have to fight against other groups to establish the existence of your own."

"To get back to the case of offshoring, reserving a company's benefits for its own people is essential."

"Because it reinforces the reality of its existence. It strengthens the fragile bonds that exist between the people that make it up."

"In an ideal world, where everyone occupies a special place enabling him to establish himself within the heart of a united group, in Complementarity with others, the place of the private company is in the middle of a complex, favouring the interests of the existence of the happy humans who work for it. It should serve the interests of the group which enabled its creation, and by the same token should provide an activity and a salary to members of that group. That is its primary function!"

"And it should be its primary goal."

"If it wants to last in its country of origin."

"The ideal world already exists in that case!"

"We live in the best possible world."

"The world is populated by people who are gathered in sub-groups who, to defend the very existence of the sub-group, challenge others to the point of offence. But beyond the rules of this great game, all connect their feelings and emotions through one medium which draws them all together: the Internet."

"All that remains is for this amazing means of communication to gain awareness like that of human understanding."

"Isn't that already the case?"

"What do you mean?"

"My guess is that the neuron which, in Complementarity with billions of others, participates in the emergence of the human conscience knows nothing, if this makes any sense, about the Consciousness which oversees the complementary group. So the Consciousness of humanity can only appear to an observer located somewhere outside of this humanity."

"And this Consciousness of humanity, is this the one your angel told you of, the one that is unique and accessible to some in the World of Ideas?"

"I'm sure of it. Just like it brings together all the sensitivity that is expressed by sharing the surface of our feelings. It inspires new, wilder concepts…"

"This exchange of ideas is also an exchange of fleeting impressions, of resentments."

"It's still a little mixed up. But this chaotic aspect indicates a presumption of an awareness of oneself. I'm sure it won't be long now. Maybe it has already happened, I don't know."

"You can't know – you're part of the process. Your judgement is imperfect, incomplete."

"And the vagaries of living with others corroborate the reality of an anthropomorphic, or just animal organism.

Just like the cells of a body adapt in Complementarity with others, sometimes in conflict to the point of destroying each other, so human beings live together. However, even more so than a simple cell, humans are capable of pooling their intelligence and their sensitivity – in a word, their humanity."

"So the Consciousness that is born of this connection between wise understandings is on a whole different level."

HAPPINESS AS THE ONLY GOAL

"For want of creating in every Consciousness the incarnation of the World of Ideas, men must work every day towards a happy attitude towards their vision of reality. In other words, they must write the story that will carry them through time. But don't you find it is harder and harder to progress in a beneficial way towards a hypothetical feelings scholarship?"

"What do you mean?"

"Well in order to find any kind of point to this great game of life on Earth, you have to create great fluctuations in the state of mind of human beings. Idleness is clearly only desirable for some. And yet many seek extreme sensations in a calm and comforting context. You have to accept being unhappy to have a chance of experiencing ecstasy!"

"While hoping, each time, to return to a state of equilibrium."

"But everyone will have a chance to experience that state in the next generation. We mustn't forget the eternal return!"

"You wouldn't feel like playing at war by any chance?"

"You know if I say 'yes', do you think that would start a Third World War? No, of course we are all force-fed the 'duty to remember'. We have all learned much from our mistakes, and we have made so many that from now on it is almost impossible for any inter-human movement to generate sufficient division in thinking that could create a state or war or something approaching it."

"And you regret that?"

"The problem is that all this violent action has moved over into the world of the virtual. Human life is now arbitrarily maintained at an unexpected level of stability."

"You mean you would rather people got killed?"

"Bearing in mind the condition and the definition of humans on Earth, it would be a wonderful way of reducing the impact of the population explosion."

"You're scaring me. And how do you suppose the situation can be fixed?"

"Through the 'duty to forget'. The possibility that an entire generation can refuse to let itself be castrated, have its wings clipped and have its ideas, born of all these past sensations, crushed."

"Artists go to war!"

"Yes, something like that…"

THE OUTSIDE WORLD

"The outside world is to a certain extent defined by the questions we ask about it." So my intuition was right. Ever since I was very young I have feared finding out the ultimate truth about the Being; the reality about that which is standing behind me. I believe there is nothing – desperately nothing.

While our Consciousnesses gambol in a mass of cloudy illusions, despite the evidence we see with our own eyes, the haziness of our knowledge gets blown in all directions. I am afraid of the truth. I fear for my reason. Everything trembles beneath the steps of a very fleeting glory: being the inventor of complacency! It's laughable.

"But if I turn round, the illusion will take shape won't it?"

Of course…

"And what of love in all this?"

"Love?"

"What I mean is that so far you simply want to reduce the number of humans living on Earth because there are too many people to your liking and it makes you uncomfortable."

"And doesn't it you?"

"No. When I'm with someone I love, everything seems to be right with the world. I suppose the problem stems from the fact that you haven't yet found the person destined for you."

"So I have to go out to meet other people with the secret desire of finding a fragment of a Consciousness that was mine in a past life."

"What do you mean?"

"This is an assumption but it is now a given that each fragment of Consciousness finds itself, upon someone's death, mixed with other pieces before a fragment born of this new blend finds itself in a novice mind. Well, it's a fairly safe bet that if two fragments that once formed just a single fragment came across each other in a new life, they would get on pretty well!"

"It would be like love at first sight."

"That's absolutely it. Haven't you ever wondered why sometimes you meet someone for the first time but feel like you already know them?"

"You mean I have already known their Consciousness?"

"More than that. Your Consciousness may have lived with theirs in someone's mind in a previous generation."

"That's great!"

"Especially since, when you think about it, if you go back a few generations there is a high chance we have something in common with most people on Earth."

"But we don't experience love at first sight with everyone."

"Of course there are thousands of smaller details that come into the equation. That is all part of geometric chaos. But in principle, there is nothing to stop anyone from becoming attached to and even loving anyone else."

"In which case, nothing on Earth could keep them from being happy."

"It would be like witnessing the privatisation of the Consciousness by its partner. The two Consciousnesses which belong to each other draw an enclosed space around themselves, a private area. It is a convincing fact of Complementarity: the two minds work together to ensure the long-lastingness of their union. They now form one single Consciousness in action, one single being."

"Wouldn't this be a way of simplifying the structure created by all these fragments of Consciousness without always having to resort to death?"

"It certainly is in the same order as altruism or philanthropy. This would be about an empathy suggested by the recognition in the other of an element complementary to one's own. It would mean organisation without repression. In fact it's ideal…"

"The organisation of man with just one guideline: Complementarity!"

"Complementarity would in fact be a conceptual transformation of the love that unites man. A little as if the similarities and differences in the other that attract us to them were simply the apparent proof of a more than formal and doubtless deeper bond which exists and persists in individuals."

"I think you are touching on a reality other prophets have already looked at. It would seem it was the only truth revealed to us by the angels. The attraction between people is the basis for communities. And these communities must defend their definition. To this end they rise up against each other and love turns to hate. But this hate is as important as love. It implies a strong interest in the other and that is what is behind all the major dynamics that have worked up human populations, inciting men to create and unconditionally strengthening the incidence of Complementarity."

"By privatising a fragment of the total Consciousness, lovers create an unbreakable bond between two Consciousnesses. This bond, placed next to others around the world, reduces the instances of scattered pieces of this martyrised Consciousness. In other words, couples who get together enable the beginning of an organisation which could lead to the general organisation recommended by Complementarity. In any case, without having to dramatically reduce the number of individuals. That's the solution!"

"So we don't take out any minds, we organise them into couples. Because people in a couple, even if it doesn't last, have parallel perceptions. So we have to get match-making!"

"Well, that's roughly it."

NEW DEAL

Sitting on the floor, in the middle of the scattered layers of my irreverent thoughts, I finally prepare to take on this ultimate challenge with pride. I am still alive, more than ever even. And I am going to share the derision that fills me in the face of this monstrous emptiness of sense.

Last night I looked back on what delighted me in my childhood. And I realised that all this was already printed in the infinite lining of every pore in my skin. I always start the same words over again. I tirelessly repeat the same vital forces. I write as I run, towards the insidious harmony of time.

What is my role here on Earth?

In the mature perfection of ideal Complementarity, I feel the enormity of that which separates us and yet remains the guarantee of human cohesion. A blossoming Consciousness, above and beyond the vulgar instances. An aura of fire to build the legend of tomorrow.

Imagine the following:

Everyone discovers their place and their role. Everyone fits into an incandescent future, working for themselves and for others. No more reminiscing about the past. We forget history and we build the foundations of a general elevation of understandings tinged with good fortune. The 'duty to forget' rises proudly over the rotting corpse of the duty of commemorative memory.

Freed from this useless clutter, the memory focuses on the essential, the absolute consciousness of complacency. Why stop ourselves from trying? Why not free ourselves from the irreversible desire for power? Together we can achieve anything. The image of our sinuous paths in the absurd traces of geometric chaos becomes fixed. It crystallises on the repugnant size of our instincts. But free our probable craving for time because we will be alive for a long time yet!

Destroy the museums! They are the memorial millstones that our civilisation drags around with it. Let us reduce to ashes the material imprints of the past. There is nothing to fear! Digital progress has rendered this memory virtual.

It is time to reform memory.

A new deal!

"You see, I understand that the major problem of the current human community is linked to its exponential expansion, and that we need to stabilise the number of Consciousnesses currently in action, if not reduce them. But it is barely acceptable to force the elderly to die sooner - even if we can justifiably believe that this death is simply a pathway to a new generation. Ideally, what should happen is that each old person, fully aware of what will happen to his own Consciousness, decides to shuffle off his mortal coil to find a newer one."

"But along with his mortal coil, he also shuffles off his memories."

"A new life is being offered to him. Tired and worn out by this one, he can in all conscience ask to rejoin the total Consciousness before being incorporated into new minds. But yes, he would typically lose the memories attached to his neural person."

"Or…"

"Or part of them will continue – partly in the minds of those who have known him and partly in an astute migration towards the Consciousness, because these sensations will go on to fuel the World of Ideas."

"So not all the memories are lost. And every life is worth living because it contributes to the source of all inspiration of new elements. These new sensations, arising from the travels of a mind through an explosion of stimuli, are the traces left in the Consciousness of humanity by the passage on Earth of an arrangement of Consciousness nestled within a mind in action. Because that is a crucial consequence of this revelation. Each of us, in the interests of Complementarity, must fulfil a role defined by our rightful place in the structure governing us and, in a certain way, provide our great human family with the very essence of our last visit on Earth."

"That gives everyone a right to act!"

"This magical consequence that can be summed up in just a few words, gives man the goal he has long searched for – a purpose in life."

"Working together to expand the field of sensations available for all those searching for inspiration – that's Complementarity's best approach."

DISILLUSION

Everyone thought they had discovered the ultimate truth, the supreme order that governed the stars beyond all human eventualities. As if we were the exception, thrust into the heart of an ordered system until it sickened us. Everyone was wrong.

Apparent order and disorder and geometric chaos go hand in hand. More than that, they are so intertwined that the one seems but a certain view of the other. And time plays to this. If we explore the life of stars over a long enough period, long enough on the scale of these celestial machines, the apparent order becomes so muddled it floats over the divine chaos.

The apparent order in these gigantic movements is but a privileged moment where everything seems to line up like a myth – like when the foam on a wave appears to reveal the face of someone who has died and plays with our memory.

We cannot and we should not try to bring order to everything.

The drive of a mind that tries to systemise things is naive. The man-child doubles up laughing at his understanding of the world. And the future rolls out the thousands of combinations that come into play. The Being is intangible because it toys with us.

What future is there for those who dream of seizing the fabulous aura of the conception of the world? A void burdened with the repugnant weight of the surrounding darkness. You need to dare to disregard the ruins of the Enlightenment. You need to accept the insidious veil of lost illusions. Everything is linked in a great access to happiness on Earth.

The Complementarity of all the actors in this play now serves as the law. It has to be officially recognised in the cosmetic eulogy of nature as the original source of shared happiness. Complementarity as an established fact, so that everything that touches us resonates in the firmament with majestic happiness.

The time of disillusionment is over!

"Imagine for a moment that you were not the only person on Earth to have just encountered an angel. And even that he may have appeared to many people lately. It's not irrational to think that out of the billions of individuals currently alive on this planet, some other than you may have received a visit. Especially as, if you think about it, your disposition to direct, rather spectacular, almost fairy-like inspiration is probably written in the definition of the Consciousness within you today."

"To start with there are doubtless all the others who are animated with a Consciousness certain aspects of which were assembled in one single body in a prior generation"

"Your potential lovers!"

"Yes, those who, having similar stimuli, will produce similar responses. Because I think if this angel came to me, it is because everything that happened beforehand meant that he could only appear in that spot."

"It's likely that others had the same luck too."

"I guess so."

"And then those people too would want to share the revelation. It's likely that two people are having a similar conversation to ours somewhere else. And if that is the case, this wonderful idea of Complementarity will progress."

"That's great!"

"But how will this affect the daily lives of individuals?"

"They will have a different attitude to death: it will not be the evil but necessary pain that many clever people try to thwart, but a restorative passage to the next generation. In becoming aware of the immortality of his essence, the enlightened man can try to nourish the biosphere with his work, knowing that he is performing transformations for the human species. He knows he is like his fellow man because we are all holders of a fragment of the total Consciousness. That will lead him to think as an individual of the same species, scattered over the same stardust in the middle of his brothers."

"That is fine regarding general behaviour and a different mentality but what concrete changes will there be in his daily life?"

"The nature of his work will change. He will no longer accept a repetitive and degrading job. He will aspire to an activity that will provide him, ideally, with the material goods to assume and develop his individuality in a protective and remunerated context. He will refuse to be exploited or threatened. His work will have to bring him a positive context as well as a pay packet."

"Only a part of his time is spent in paid work; what about his leisure time?"

"Within his leisure activities he needs to find occupations that will enable him to accomplish his destiny. They must be creative and artistic and enable him to experience again that ease with which as a child he accessed the World of Ideas and found inspiration. But this tendency to play with divine inspiration should be exploited in all aspects of daily life."

"And even if he is single-minded, he will make his main activity a total expression of his creativity!"

"In that regard, the artist is the most rounded of all men in his quest for Complementarity"

"Yes, but this qualification encompasses all active people who, in their activity, seek to welcome as a child would the deified world of sensations and ideas, the inspiration to create new shapes and new concepts. Whether he is a musician, a writer or a basic seeker, it is in the search for new combinations of concepts that passed through the total Consciousness before coming to him, that the artists offer the world a singularly systematic progress."

"So there are a number of hidden artists?"

"All minds which temporarily host a fragment of the single Consciousness, conducive to managing those working with it for creative purposes, in other words the development of new forms and ideas likely to aid mankind progress in time, are artists."

"And everyone has a vocation to be so."

"Naturally."

"Well there's something that should give idle hands a reason to be active and creative by using their own individuality."

"Because each of us is unique and each must add his stone to the communal building that is the human species. That is what enables this entity lost in the cosmos to evolve sustainably over time."

QUANTUM PHYSICS

All forms of knowledge translate into automatic reflexes unique to a species. All interest in a topic of study reveals the insidious presence of two states of the entity. Words can only cling to that reality incorporated as such in each human mind: onto each entity is grafted the origins of two dynamics, one centrifugal, and the other centripetal. And what is at the origin of units and categories reveals the importance of human reasoning in its particular condition. Everything that surrounds us, near or far, is at some point a topic of conversation. And as such, it is tainted by indelible traces left on it by human interpretation.

A pared down form of this dishonest system appears, however, in the study of the infinitely small.

Although nothing can blur the objective purity of the entities that are topics of conversation, the appearance of the latter is shrouded in a doubt as to the real nature of these objects. They appear by turn and even together in a centripetal form - the particle - and in a centrifugal form - the wave.

There is enough in that for us to understand the perverse nature of our principle means of comparison.

It is a sad reality.

"It is sometimes edifying to see a group form around a pretext that is either false or of such a size as to make you want to smile."

"I see what you mean."

"These ephemeral groups pepper human activity. They are a reflection of a lost quest to reconquer the unity which dominates us. Indeed, within these groups men find a communion of feelings. They can forget themselves as individuals and let themselves be guided by a fragment of Consciousness superior to their own sketched out above them. Far from being the sum of all these Consciousnesses put into play, the group often reveals itself incapable in the face of the social values present in each one of us."

"That leaves them wide open to excess."

"These groups are often the result of a burst of sentimentality, as if the excess of feeling upset reasoning. They become out of control, deaf to reason. Only primary instincts survive."

"Are they inspired by Complementarity too?"

"They are missing a basic element of Complementarity: effective adjustment. And to create that, men group together without seeking to organise or adjust themselves. Yet Complementarity requires people to commit themselves fully to their project and a profitable exchange of the skills in play."

"Do you need to be aware of what you are participating in?"

"You have to act with full knowledge of the facts. You have to agree to integrate an advantageous space where you can express your personality and act in accordance with it, in a calm but provoking environment."

"Provoking what?"

"What I mean is that this environment seems calm but nevertheless it stirs up the most creative layer of the Consciousness. It's not a calmness that leads to a numbing of the senses but one which arouses them."

"So we are conscious of the reality."

"Unlike the lucky groups which jump on the bandwagon of ephemeral happiness, Complementarity requires the Consciousness to control the effects of that. This enables you to develop your individuality within a united group."

"Which also enables you to be happy over the long-term."

"That's right. It's the ideal 21st century life."

PROBABLE RECONSTITUTION

We are more than brothers. We share with other conscious beings on Earth the universal origins of this superior entity, the Consciousness of the human being. Like the scattered fragments of a shattered sphere, we all strain to rediscover a little of this uniqueness. And associations of individuals offer us a glimpse of this vast pleasure that is Complementarity.

And it begins with the effective coming together of bodies in the act of love-making. Two become one and the orgasm which liberates this revitalising energy is for our own good. Human gatherings add to this offer of happiness a feeling of belonging to a group where we can lose our individuality and recover the uniqueness of the superior class. Associations of ideas or characteristics also arouse a similar happiness within us. It is only the intensity or the stakes that change.

So rather than an ultimate ideology, a new aesthetic of thought is taking shape. After having abandoned our more or less agreed illusions, we will consciously choose to commit our energy to the construction of a new religion. This will aim to generate a shared happiness in the development of multiple individualities in a united and solid group. The Complementarity thus generated will contribute to supplying fragments of the total Consciousness with the tangible idea of this shared origin.

Because the aware man is but a fragment of this total Consciousness and he yearns to rebuild it.

"But how do you envisage an individual developing their individuality – something which tends to isolate him within the tumult of active personalities, while integrating himself into a process based on Complementarity?"

"It's not a contradiction in terms. The individual acquires their own characteristics which give them their own personality. Once this personality has found its ideal place, it can insert itself in complete Complementarity with those around it. This isn't about levelling out a people. Equality, by the way, is a forbidden concept. This is about bringing personalities together like in a puzzle, to approach the reconstituted image of a unique understanding made up of fundamentally different elements. Once that has been accomplished, everyone is of equal importance because everyone upholds the structure built on the concept of Complementarity in the same way. There is no more hierarchy, only individuals, all different, all unequal, working together to develop and strengthen the being of their group."

"So these different and unequal individuals are pieces of a puzzle which represent the complex structure of the group."

"That's right. They have to arrange themselves in such a way as to form a coherent and solid structure. But in that arrangement, each piece is useful. There are no useless or surplus individuals. People organise themselves for a while, come together to practice an aesthetic of life, a mentality. Then, when they have reached the end of their useful function, they make a conscious decision to withdraw."

"To return in the next generation…"

"In order that the fragment of Consciousness that animates them can rejoin the World of Ideas before temporarily rejoining a new and still naive mind, stripped of memories and feelings that had just recently been shared. The cycle repeats itself endlessly."

"Thus goes the cycle of incarnations!"

"But it's clear that the new fragment of Consciousness taken from the totality will rarely be similar to the old one that just joined it. In between the two events everything is blended together again."

"You mean a child will very rarely receive a big part of the Consciousness of a deceased person, big enough to be recognisable?"

"It's very rare indeed, because beforehand, the Consciousness which animates the deceased is melted into the totality."

"But some lumps might get through…"

THE TELLTALE DOUBT

"I find it difficult to believe all this. In fact I am convinced that this whole mass of hypothesis is nothing more than the fruit of the over liberal workings of your mind based on a few words that popped into your head and that you think were spoken by an angel."

"Don't you believe me?"

"I believe that your delirium is legitimate, as are all the deliriums of prophets. Your reasoning draws on the best reasoning of humanity so why not? Your thought process holds up. And it has the merit of producing a positive momentum for the happiness of mankind and the planet. It should enable people to live and also die more happily. So I am willing to accept this ultimate illusion that you call Complementarity."

"But the fact that you consider it an illusion surely robs it of some of its power of persuasion."

"I think that humanity is sufficiently mature now to accept its intrinsic inaptitude to grasp one single idea of the Being. It can accept living in a semantic blur and it can knowingly choose to draw inspiration from the most modern of life ethics."

"Complementarity."

"Since this offers nothing but advantages, both individual happiness and happiness the planet over, there shouldn't be much problem convincing the most reluctant."

"Don't believe it! Because what I am suggesting here would replace beliefs that people have signed up to whole-heartedly. A religion is much more than just a teaching. It demands total adhesion. And it is difficult to give up that which you have accepted your entire life without displaying a little doubt."

"And yet it would be so good for humanity to discover the primary meaning of religion - that of bringing mankind together in a single momentum to benefit from the advantages of community life and progress towards a shared happiness."

"That's right: one single religion for the human community, one single progressive dynamic, one single upward impetus. But the happiness you speak of goes hand in hand with equal sorrow. It is not happiness that should guide us but the accentuated contours of emotions and feelings so that life is more intense."

"To listen to you, one would think you were nostalgic for past wars when courage and heroism could transform the life of an individual into a real adventure!"

"Don't forget that we all have within us a part of our being that already lived through all that. It's clear we have already benefited from it. And it made life that much more interesting. Our ultimate plan was the realisation of an ideal, not predictable decrepitude. Being aware of the reality of the journey in fragments of the Consciousness over the generations, we should be more ready to risk death with neither fear nor sadness. The reality is that other younger minds will follow on after our bodies – which are destined to disappear - and house the scattered Consciousness. Evidently nothing serious is happening to our planet. And even death offers another chance to play at life. Everything's fine!"

"Are you looking to inscribe the individual in a temporality beyond his own generation?"

"But that's already the case isn't it?"

"OK, we all have within us a part of this humanity which prevails over us, but as we develop, we also forge an ego which doesn't leave us until we die. And it's this ego which is at the heart of this imperial need we feel to be individual. And it is also the sad cause of us forgetting the true nature of our being and our intimate relationship with other conscious beings."

"If that ego is with us throughout our life, the reality of our being does not vanish. And religion should remind us we are all alike and complementary because we all have within us a fragment of a single Consciousness. But in the age of the Internet which is linking us all together, religion has to become unique again to link the profound convictions of all conscious beings on Earth."

"That's not going to be easy. There are still too many differences between beliefs. And some people are too attached to them."

"I sincerely think things are beginning to change at an exponential speed. With the Internet, people are forgetting their traditions and immersing themselves in a reconstituted global Consciousness."

"I'm ready to believe you."

SALUTARY REACTION

Of course the global warming we are currently experiencing on Earth is caused by an external factor, i.e. the sun. Of course we cannot do anything about it. But at the dawn of a new era where rationality has for a large part superseded superstition, it is impossible for us to recognise our inability to control our destiny. Otherwise it would have been easy to put ourselves in the hands of several giant hominoids. It would have been salutary for our reactivity to have prayed to them in the best case scenario or offered human or animal sacrifices in the worst. Because it is in our constitution, as in that of every living being to react to multiple stimuli in proportion to their effect on us.

So, failing a belief in a rational system too, failing a broad understanding of the causes and effects at an interstellar level, we have chosen to react by trying to control the uncontrollable.

Two mice shut up in a cage with an electrified floor will end up killing each other. And when even war does not allow us to burn off all the excess energy that the divine stimulus generates in us, something else has to be found. Then there is the myth of climate change being caused by our little car or our daily journey. When you take a good look at it, our impact is laughable compared to the prodigious torrent of carbon dioxide sent out into the atmosphere by the smallest of volcanoes. But worse still, it is quite plain that it is the global warming of the planet that is causing an increase in CO_2 levels and not the reverse.

But there, we have to react in one way or another. Just don't forget, once one of the mice has died, the remaining mouse curls up and waits, inert, for the end of the unpleasant stimulus or death.

So, faced with the great unknown in which we cannot reasonably count for much, let us debate this over and over. But certainly not to the detriment of immediate happiness which remains the sole justification for our existence on Earth.

"I've understood a lot of things. I have evolved since last time. I've acquired a sense of the ephemeral."

"What do you mean by that?"

"Paradoxically, the immutability of the singleness of the Consciousness's diaphanous veil revealed to me the impermanence of all that is."

"Everything changes over time. Beings are born, live and die. Even objects fade after having shined with utility."

"We have to start by accepting it, accepting that everything comes to an end at some point. We live in the middle of a universe in progress, which is transforming and evolving. We really mustn't try to stop this flight of time. We would be greatly disappointed. Only the World of Ideas is unchangeable."

"And yet, in the West especially, new museums are springing up packed with works that we never stop trying to restore. It's a waste of time isn't it?"

"The only route to perpetuity is to transfer to the World of Ideas."

"What do you mean?"

"The accumulated feelings in the World of Ideas, the single Consciousness, is not doomed to disappear. The treatment of feelings is out of human hands. However there is another way which appears to have a foothold in the doorway of posterity: digitisation which, in the absence of a comprehensive back-up system, can claim to save a large number of visible elements of an object from decay. But for the moment this only really applies to sound and images, two favoured senses."

"A digital work saved from the throes of putrefaction."

"In theory, yes."

"And what will become of the museums?"

"It is fundamentally prejudicial to the future of humanity in the same way as the damaging 'duty to remember' which we would like to replace with a 'duty to forget', to preserve in the controlled atmosphere of museums the supposed paragons of perishable beauty. Imagine the freedom we would regain if all these examples, so often restored, were not hindering our will to try again!"

"On the contrary. I think that for us, beyond being models to follow, they are the guarantee of an inexhaustible source of inspiration and artistic orientation. From the old comes forth the new and modern."

"Except if, for inspiration, we refer exclusively back to the stored history of sensations and ideas of this world blessed by gods that the museums feed us with so parsimoniously."

"If I have understood you correctly, you want all the works to be destroyed, or rather abandoned to the perishable state of material goods and that the creativity of artists should only be inspired by digital memory?"

"The virtual, digital space is indeed a substitute for the perfect World of Ideas and Feelings, built and controlled by the human being on Earth. It corroborates the idea of a materialisation of the dreamlike attributes of humanity. The total Consciousness reappears through the exponential development of information networks. And the complete and perfect memory of humanity, nourished by the Consciousnesses in transit which free up the sum of intimate feelings and innovative ideas stored during just one life on Earth, is roughly materialised in the bytes of available memory."

"It leads one to conclude that men are rebuilding their own essence, creating an image of their truth, their god!"

"Humanity continues a work that is dear to it: managing to build on Earth a valid representation of the miraculous system that created it."

"It is as if the image were printed in a collective unconsciousness and that everyone must imperatively take part in the establishment of a template of this image by acting in Complementarity."

"Then everything can be explained! The role of everyone is clear. The purpose of life is there. All of us poor ants lost in a world we don't understand must act together to build on Earth a naive representation of the miraculous system to which we belong. That is our common goal."

"We are now beginning to glimpse at the general shape of this gigantic Lego set. We can begin to hope that humanity, linked by the result of progress in communication, the Internet, will understand all this soon. But perhaps it's already the case. Humanity has become aware. And the ultimate human creation is taking shape. With the addition of the digital memory, which caricatures a World of Ideas only accessible to the most talented, the copy is almost perfect. Although it remains a copy."

"Like a child caricatures its parents, nubile humanity, in aiming for an exponential development of the digital, creates a pastiche of its god."

THE DYNAMIC OF BOREDOM

I think this time I really need to be in agreement with myself. I simply need to explain what I believe I know.

Something like the imperial, infantile delirium of a certain glory on Earth. Whatever! Why not a messiah while we're about it? That kind of delirium has to stop. There really is little chance that all this reality should be anything other than a fantastic combination of factors. We'll come back to that.

But in the case of the probable, how do we organise our instincts to accomplish that which all those who have preceded us have instructed us to do? Why would we continue to showcase this pain assigned by the sum of human acts?

I am afraid of finally taking the easy way by declaring myself beaten and falling into line with the will of the tribe. I hate this tribe that obsesses me, that leaves me full of doubt faced with the options apparently freely praised by my angel.

I doubt everything.

I doubt myself.

How is this going to end?

"Once you have has grasped the obsequious necessity of the technical development that necessarily goes hand-in-hand with the imitation of divine mechanisms, it becomes a requirement for man to maintain – even augment – this momentum which inhabits him and those like him."

"You mean we have found the meaning of life?"

"Perhaps yes…"

"So if man manages to recreate the global Consciousness on Earth by linking every human being, linking their ideas and feelings, they will be able to recreate the imaginary paradise?"

"If mankind manages to act in Complementarity, more than that even, the product of their labour will enable their dearest wish to come true, the association of all minds with a view to the emergence of a single Consciousness on Earth."

"And will that make them happy?"

"At least it will cancel the latent despair created by the excessive growth of the population. Human beings, all united in their intimacy, will be able to define their path towards the constitution of a fraternal unity likely to let individualities develop."

"But there will still be as many incidences of sorrow as of joy, both on a human community and an individual level?"

"Obviously that would be desirable. People have to accept that and use it to develop the general point of the great game of life."

"Do you think humanity is still in its infancy when it plays at imitating its creator?"

"It imitates what is written deep in its Consciousness, a sort of technical diagram of the intimate workings of the Being."

"We shouldn't try to interfere with its work. On the contrary, with all our body and soul we should try to facilitate its expression."

"That's it. Those who have managed to find their place in society, who are able to occupy it in Complementarity with others and who also take part in their first joint project, i.e. linking people to each other and making their common memory long-lasting, are the most likely to experience tangible happiness."

"A happiness which has to be accompanied by an equal sorrow."

"This happiness will be more of the serene kind, a well-being. But I would imagine it being interspersed with moments of unhappiness followed by other types of worries or grief. Anyway, it would be a pleasant experience."

"In Complementarity, is there not a mechanism similar to that which has existed for a long time in solidarity or fraternity?"

"Solidarity supposes the existence of a caste system which governs relations between those who help and those who are helped. And even if the relations can be reversed, that has little to do with Complementarity which presupposes an equal treatment of conditions. Also, there is a goal to our Complementarity, while solidarity can occur simply in a state."

"You mean solidarity implies mutual aid based on need while Complementarity is based on a common plan, a goal which defines the momentum, the general dynamic?"

"That's right. While fraternity gives the impression of being the beginnings of Complementarity."

"How so?"

"Well, a brotherhood contains the premises of all the consecutive elements of Complementarity. Because brothers know how to shape themselves with regards to each other in the interests of equal benefit while each strengthens their being."

"They have a shared goal."

"Yes. During their shared life, they apply themselves to activities, as a couple, by acting together in a place they have defined during their activity. That doesn't mean there won't be tension. But they will manage to overcome it for the sake of their goal, the strongest of forces. So they can accommodate a difference of opinion that favours the development of innovative ideas."

111

"So in fraternal relations there is a particular consideration for the other that you would like to see in people living together within a society based on the Complementarity of its members?"

"That's right. Each one in their rightful place develops their abilities and their individuality in the pursuit of a common goal, by drawing on the work of others and sharing the best of themselves via the work they provide."

"Like brothers."

"With the addition of the prior definition of a common outcome, like a legendary quest for Heaven on Earth!"

"Which implies that dissention may occur. The life of a brotherhood is never entirely stress-free. Conflicts regularly arise but are just as quickly resolved because more than rivalries and differences can divide, the same origins can unite."

"Like brothers, the people of Earth sharing a common origin."

"And that similar origin is the engine room of their coexistence, the inspirer of the unbreakable *rapprochement* which drives their relationship."

THE WORLD OF IDEAS

"Listen, I think there's something really interesting here. Complementarity should replace all other attempts to organise society. It's a great method. If everyone manages to find the spot that is intended for him, intended because it is unique in the race for perfection, then everyone can live happily, that is serenely, in a society whose main goal is ultimately to reproduce the absolute on Earth."

"It's a pity that calls into question a fair few founding principles of some communities."

"Are you thinking of religions, or some religions?"

"Obviously it is difficult to ask those most steeped in religiousness to forget the tales written in books when their entire lives have been based on a chance interpretation of a few lines of writing from the depths of time."

"And yet there's a strong chance this is the solution to our problems. In fact, if everyone recognised the validity of this system, they would then rediscover the force of a source of communal inspiration and would be able to approach the future unfettered."

"What do you mean?"

"Out of the many religions which oppose mankind by claiming theirs is the only way, humanity could finally build a single dogma that would unite everyone in the same progressive momentum. Then they would be free to concentrate fully on their ultimate destiny: creating Heaven on Earth!"

"So now you have everything you need to live happily on Earth, a clear and valid final goal, the means to achieve it and a metaphysical context which enables it."

"Most of all I have the instinct favoured of all adventurers. My Consciousness must have accompanied a good many in previous generations. I am ready to dedicate this life to making this idea reality."

"The angel picked on the right person."

"He did it in full knowledge of the facts. This time he needed an emblematic prophet with a fantastic aura. He needed a man who had nothing to lose in this life and who was in complete disaccord with this futile consumer society which generates servile beings who forget to think."

"But weren't you born into this society?"

"Yes but I come from a different planet remember? Like the Little Prince, I landed one morning amongst a people who had stopped thinking."

"That's a bit hard. The people you mix with are only the divided reminiscences of courageous individuals who have already lived. They suffer from this state of affairs too but you despise them!"

"That really wasn't my intention. On the contrary, I want to unite them behind this fabulous project. But we have to hurry before the demographic explosion creates even more obstacles."

"Like what for example?"

"By dint of diluting man's share of the total Consciousness, people start forgetting where they come from. They maintain their childhood naivety until death. And their life lacks utility to say the least."

"Humanity is regressing?"

"As its size increases, so the point of the universal project for the most part diminishes. Only a few manage to thwart the foreseeable decline, and we're lucky even they do."

"Since the beginning of time it is people who are ordinary in their being but extraordinary in their acts who have led the community of men towards their destiny!"

"But up until now they never sought to create a carbon copy of the perfect World of Ideas on Earth. Humanity as a child persisted in projecting its desires into a space detached from the biosphere. By inventing a post-mortem heaven, man detached himself from the responsibilities incumbent upon him."

"Such as?"

"Responsibility for his immediate environment. But that's all part of the game. You can't know the end from the start. I suppose that it is only now, once the process has been pretty much set in motion, that we can at last reveal the purpose of all this."

"Since almost everyone is now connected to each other by the Internet, it is now clear that this process, the full magnitude of which is now apparent, is the result of a will shared by all conscious individuals who have found some sort of unity."

"And this unity is the recurring theme of an almost obvious reality, the subject of the revelation."

"There is only one Consciousness, only one!"

"We could have worked that out long ago if we hadn't been blinded by the illusions inherited from another time."

"Religions?"

"Yes. Evidently I had to detach myself from them to a large degree before an angel dared come near me."

"But you can't be the only one then?"

"There is a significant chance that yes, elsewhere, similar revelations may have been made to an individual curious and adventurous enough to accept the unexpected presence of a talking diaphanous veil."

"Then again, maybe the encounter occurred but the budding prophet didn't understand all the implications of such a simple syntactic turn. Because you have to add a considerable degree of maieutics to it to unlock the very source of a new mentality."

"It's an absolute precondition."

Consumer society is on its last legs. Commerce as it has developed so far, finds itself faced with its own insolent fatuity. The very idea of inscribing the foundations of an existence on Earth on a frenzied quest for power through one single medium, praised as universal – i.e. money – puts those worried about the absolute in chains. And yet, all you need to do is look at the void being dug between globalisation's idea of what we need to be happy and the material reality of such a quest. Obviously the key to happiness does not lie in the accumulation of manufactured goods. Quite the opposite.

So what should we do with this excess of materialism, with all these objects that insidious commerce offers us by teaching us the art of desire until it makes us sick? Because that is the case. Advertising models our appetite for the useless. So we are forced to consume, not out of need or desire but out of disappointment. These objects which martyrise our innermost hope for Complementarity and thus fraternity cannot continue to occupy our primitive functions.

And what if finally, by a universal programmed revelation, everyone became aware of the tragic reality of things? New man, now free of the hateful occupations that fill the existence of a born consumer, can throw himself into a new life, a happy life which requires only the minimum of material goods and which finally takes an interest in the very basics of Complementarity.

Production will lose its usefulness. Why produce anything above and beyond what is strictly necessary? And human enterprises will at last officially become what they always have been despite the urban myths so deeply embedded in our consumerist anxieties.

The primary purpose of a company is to provide its staff with a salary. In other words, to offer staff employment and financial reward. The more a company offers interesting employment for a good wage, the more popular it becomes. In order to continue in this role, it is handy if the occupation is sellable, or the products arising from it are, so that this money can be put back into staff wages.

Also, it is obvious that a company is of interest to the members of the community where it operates. And thus we see the indisputable absurdity of offshoring. How come we didn't think of this before?

Happiness is born of effective recognition of the Complementarity of all the machinery of human activity.

"What is the point of the game if men live in perfect harmony and the greatest peace? Are we not then approaching idleness, in which case all existence becomes useless as it is impervious to all feeling?"

"Which is why it is so important to preserve the initial antagonisms of new types of feelings."

"Complementarity, like fraternity by the way, enables rivalries and opposition to take root in human relations. And that's a good thing because it activates a state of mind favourable to creativity. Apathy of the senses hinders these moments of divine inspiration."

"So if I understand correctly, we need to seek out confrontation and struggles for the completion of our being, or risk our creativity stagnating in futile repetition."

"That's absolutely right. You need to have a reason to motivate your inventiveness. And what better reason that that of confronting someone who aspires to a social status that the completion of your personality has enabled you to attain?"

"Is there no other way of inspiring your own creativity?"

"Because of their antagonistic dynamics, falling out and making up encourage movement and therefore the basis of creation. Out of sensitive altercations are born the useful intentions to take action to make real that which the muses have inspired in us. Love and hate are the vectors of a sensitive focalisation likely to provoke a resurgence of intention to produce a work."

"I don't understand."

"If love is the inspiration, the artist will find the necessary reasons to create in his loved one."

"And if hate is the inspiration?"

"It's exactly the same process. Both excite the same mechanisms. Both refer to a strong interest in another person. And it's likely that the root cause of this interest lies in a previous fusion in the same mind of the two fragments of Consciousness now in play."

"You mean the two individuals were one in a previous life?"

"The idea that their Consciousnesses may have lived together in a single understanding is rather a romantic vision don't you think?"

"But it that actually reality?"

"I find such a hypothesis pretty well explains remarkable events which tend to be classified in a way which betrays a notorious inability to otherwise characterise them. How can you seek to understand supernatural or paranormal phenomena without resorting to an unbreakable bond between the minds that witnessed them?"

"A sort of collective hypnosis?"

"More than that. I think that physical reality is only one facet of reality. There is something more. And this magical thing is certainly linked to this Consciousness that animates a great many of us. The fact that this Consciousness is a single entity, and that its scattered fragments inhabit our minds, is the most beautiful hypothesis. It's also the simplest and most obvious. It means we can forget the dustbin categories where we stuffed everything we didn't understand, because if this is reality, it explains everything. Isn't that how we validate a hypothesis?"

"So it's not a collective hypnosis as such, but rather something like a modified state of this fragment of Consciousness that animates us all, in perfect symbiosis with all the fragments."

"So it seems obvious to you too now that it's true?"

"If you are right, and you have just proven that you have every reason to believe this to be so, then the dynamic which involves all human relations, the engine room of all life on Earth, the objective reality of the necessary *rapprochement* which must lead to Complementarity with others, this momentum common to all is what we call love."

"You have just found what must be the only defendable argument in the eyes of today's society. It's not money in a purely economic system, a value system set up by old shopkeepers blinded by their need for recognition, but the *rapprochement* of Consciousnesses on the principles of Complementarity which should guide human choice. It is time to rediscover the sole value that can claim to be at the root of all life on Earth!"

"In an ideal society, money is just a practical way of facilitating exchanges. What really binds people together is the *rapprochement* of minds seeking to build a solid structure in which each will find their place and defend it. This arrangement of will can take shape in Complementarity. It alone should govern the momentum in us."

"But to ensure this society is not the cradle of the laziness that is so damaging to evolutionary ambition, we must encourage internal conflict; tensions that will give rise to remarkable advances! We need both a comforting balance and an exciting imbalance. That's too much of a paradox!"

"No it's not because that which brings us together at one point may push us apart at another. There is little between love and hate. It is the same thing even, the interest in the other, which produces two effects which appear to be in conflict but which are never really separated."

"You mean in a society which bases itself globally on the principles of Complementarity, these dissentions will necessarily arise in the interests of the individuals and their fellow man?"

"Evidently! In any case, we needn't worry about such a community of individuals sinking into the gnawing complexities of static passions. Everything points to the opposite: that by dint of working in an environment which enables everyone to develop their own individuality in a fraternal context, the personalities, strengthened by constant encouragement, will undoubtedly end up challenging each other."

"Then won't we end up with a society that pretty much resembles the current one, with disagreements and differences of opinion creating chronic instability, all within a stable and solid structure?"

"The fundamental difference is that in our ideal society, no-one is barred from their innermost function. Everyone occupies a place which suits them and which safeguards their assets."

"But before we find our ideal place, indecision about your ambitions really resembles what people are living through now."

"So you would say there's not much to change really, just a collective awareness of the very definition of life in society, this life so special that it involves feeling this unusual *rapprochement* that animates us in the face of the interplanetary void?"

"There's a little of that undoubtedly…"

"Well I think there really is a card to play here. At a time when we're bogged down in a 'duty to remember' which drags us endlessly back to the aborted attempts of the past, ideals are regarded with suspicion. We consciously avoid building a future based on extreme concepts. But what we have here is not a subversive extreme, quite the opposite! It repeats, while presenting things from a new angle, the best of what has been said in the past in other parts of the world."

"So it would be the ideal religion, a current of universal thought which would unite humans in a block in the face of a meaninglessness that is a little too close for comfort."

"A block, but not a uniform one. Individuals can confront each other and argue and finally enable guidelines for the next generation to emerge."

"In the end, this rather desperate attempt to create on Earth a faithful copy of the innermost and idealised workings of the coherence of human Consciousnesses is also the effective reconciliation of all beliefs."

"Is that all?"

"Well, if you consider there is nothing solid on which to base a methodical study of the concrete reality of the human condition, than it is perfectly valid to begin a study based on the well-known effects of divine inspirations."

"You mean those that have inspired the major religions?"

"Yes. And the message was similar every time: to live happily on this planet, forsaken in the cosmos, we have to come together."

"Until the day when, freed from the shackles of these same religions, it finally becomes possible to settle on a fair and equitable reflection for all, based on the indications provided so far."

"Which is what we've just done!"

ORTHOTHANASIA

"I basically like this system but there is one aspect that shakes my innermost convictions."

"What's that?"

"Regarding death, or to be exact, the end of life that in this model would be controlled if not precipitated. That's what we call Orthothanasia."

"First of all it's important to remember the exact words of the revelation. There is only one Consciousness means, more than anything, it is immortal and therefore transmittable from generation to generation."

"But people become attached to fragments of this Consciousness. And it's difficult, if not impossible, to find that Consciousness again and we miss it. That's the root of the deep sadness that can engulf us."

"And you think that's a good enough reason to keep a seriously deteriorated nervous system alive beyond all reason? Once you have grasped the immortal nature of the Consciousness that inhabits it, you will want to free it of this morbid packaging so it can return to the total Consciousness before being sent out again into many younger bodies, thus continuing the human cycle of life."

"But you lose a certain arrangement of matter that you had come to love with only a slender possibility of seeing it in a new life."

"There is also the possibility that this person you were so attached to shared with you that which formed in an earlier generation one single fragment of Consciousness. And that was the main reason you got on so well. There's a high chance that this meeting was far from improvised and that a similar occurrence could well take place in the near future."

"Then there is nothing to fear about death, just a momentary separation, like losing a trump card from your hand?"

"That's about it, yes. And that is why, having lived a good life – I mean after having tested all the advantages offered by our bodies which are now nearing the end of their regenerative capacity - it is in our own interest and that of the whole of mankind on Earth, to agree to destroy ourselves so that our sensorial memory can rejoin the sensorial memory of humanity. This memory, accessible to the luckiest among us, will inspire many more people in other times."

"And this fragment of Consciousness, having downloaded its memory, can then find a new place in this obsessive masquerade that is life on Earth, by temporarily joining one or several adolescent minds."

"Orthothanasia should then be the final present an elderly person at peace with themselves offers all humanity, by enabling his finished life to enrich the fabulous collections of human sensitivity, and in allowing his Consciousness to rejoin the uniqueness of his origins before its inevitable renewal in young minds."

"Such instances of lives filled with passion right to the end should delight every adventurer who offers theirs for a full scale test. I'm willing to bet that once the majority have offered up their passions, we won't be far from Heaven on Earth. I can dream."

"And I'll walk that path with you with great pleasure. I am starting to dream too about the likely construction on our planet of an almost perfect copy of the single Consciousness thanks to the Internet. I am beginning to imagine the eternal conservation of humanity's memory thanks to digitisation. I can envisage the introduction of a welcome coherence in the heart of the human community, a harmony of alert and sharp minds playing together and having fun like brothers."

"These men will be half gods because by linking together they will enable the total Consciousness to emerge in the living world."

"If it makes you happy to call them that!"

"It's vital that the elderly let go and agree to offer their fragment to youngsters. That way a rejuvenated humanity will once again have a taste for adventures and challenges. It will stop wallowing in a futile dead end of possession."

"And the number of fragments of Consciousness, which unfortunately are gradually getting smaller, will stop increasing exponentially to fill new minds after leaving old ones."

"But tell me, if people are linking up with each other through technology, do we still need to reduce their number?"

"We have to present things differently. When man recognises that within his physical body is an eternal fragment attached to the total, he will be more willing to release it by dying to enable it to inhabit others beings in other times."

"What you mean then is that it's in the logical continuity of humanity that he should be made aware of such a reality to combat the demographic explosion? That's a bit pretentious of you don't you think?"

"All of it is pretentious if it turns out to be far from the reality. But our reasoning will function as a valid excuse. It would be a great pity in any case if we had made a mistake…"

"What are you going to do now?"

"I need to write all this down so I can share it. Don't you think it's worth it?"

"Yes, of course."

"And you don't think it will have an effect on the state of mind of aware people who get wind of it?"

"Listen, I support what you're doing. It's clear that it was you the angel spoke to. But could it have been any other way? I think that if you listened to him this morning, it was because you had prepared yourself for that. All these endless seconds that have stretched out since you first became aware, and even beforehand, contributed to

129

making you ready. This morning, in the station you know so well, a blinding light was thus able to stun your cowardly mind and set off chemical reactions in the depth of your brain making you open to a prophetic dream. You were the audience for this fantastical production. But deep inside you, you were also the author. Now there is a final reason to hope that this fabulous Complementarity will today inspire all leaders of men as well as princes. How could it be otherwise? You were born here like so many others. You received the same education as them. You were lulled by the same official illusions. I cannot conceive that you were the only one this revelation happened to!"

"No two men are identical. While their genetic code may be similar, their story is intimately personal. And this story prints its particularities in the tangle of electric tensions, mechanical connections and chemical reactions within each person's brain, and determines the very definition of each individual. I am therefore a unique person with my own story and my adventure this morning is no doubt one of a kind."

"No doubt, but I imagine there are other ways of reaching this simple and wonderful conclusion."

"I think all this has already been written down in many books. The only interest this time is that it is echoed wonderfully in the technological progress that has revealed the shared but hidden intentions of all humanity.

By enabling everyone to communicate with each other, the Internet has revealed to the world the complementary nature of the fragments of Consciousness that all men share."

"A willingness to gather together around one single will, one single Consciousness arising out of the geometric chaos – that's great!"

"And what's even greater, as you said, is that we are all susceptible to being contacted by an angel, if only we can imagine it. And what was revealed to me is already buried deep in our brains, like fuel waiting for the spark that will overturn our normal way of thinking. In my case, it has spiced up our conversation no end. But all it needs is the mind of an adventurer, a mind that rejects all preconceptions and measures all assertions from all over to see this simple formula swell to incredible proportions.

"It's the ultimate revelation!"

"The one everyone knows so well."

"So society will have to be restructured to include it in its very foundations."

"But isn't that already the case? Doesn't society already rely on the agreeable effects of a *rapprochement* inscribed in the genetic definition of mankind?"

"But Complementarity is more than a simple *rapprochement*. It also involves finding an adequate place for yourself within the heart of this society, a place you will defend, claim and proclaim…"

"That should enable all citizens to individualise themselves within a united group!"

"And we can imagine all these individuals who share more than one common identity, the various fragments of the same shattered sphere, seeking to put it back together again by sharing the effects of their sensitivity with as many people as possible who are able to add the specificities of their personality to finish building their future by coming together in a complementary way. There's enough there to envisage a radiant future for this biosphere lost in the cosmos."

"Not forgetting Orthothanasia which offers those who have already given all they can to contribute to purifying and rejuvenating the human community on Earth."

"See what a great future lays in store for the dying!"

"Much better indeed than that which obliged them to assume a status for eternity that pretty much resembles an indolence that is unreal, banal and barely agreeable."

AT THE EXTREMITY OF A HISTORY COMMON TO ALL GENERATIONS

"You know, I don't want an ordinary life this time."

"Why do you say that? Do you remember your previous ones?"

"It's not that. It's just I would so like to find the place that is mine. I feel this inner momentum drawing me upwards. I can't be satisfied with the life that's been prepared for me. I can't be satisfied with consuming. What an awful word!"

"It's up to you to ensure your existence reflects more than the sickening glare of a life without meaning. You have all the aces. You have everything you need to succeed against all probability. It's up to you to exist beyond your existence."

"But the numerous constraints spineless little people put on me exhaust me. Why do I have to make such an effort while they unpick, stitch be stitch, every wonderful idea that comes to me."

"Because that's your destiny!"

"You're kidding."

"Yes, a little. What I want to say is that this fervour that fills you is in no way futile. It's a sign of the brave. Your role is conditioned in this troubled time. You must pull yourself together!"

"I suppose you're right. Complementarity is a wonderful emblem behind which all the most enlightened of us can rally. It's the first reform of metaphysics in harmony with technological progress. There's got to be something to play with in that hasn't there?"

"I prefer that idea."

"But there's no point to this new system of values unless it's shared by as many people as possible. And how am I going to convince the most reluctant, those who are still steeped in a ceremonial religiousness? They'll certainly put up a fight."

"But didn't we reach the conclusion that all the well-known effects of this new argument were in agreement with all ethics, even those of the most controversial religions?"

"It's effects, yes. But the transcendent principles on which Complementarity is based do not go hand in hand with the official illusions of millennia-old religions. They are completely different to some. These empirical illusions have developed on the intimate experience of the memory which reminds us of the past experience of the other. Thus the deceased can claim immortality in its manifest form in the memory of the living."

"But other religions in other regions imagine a completely different reality, which draw some conclusions that have much in common with our new interpretation."

"So on the one hand we have Western religions which offer a good deal on the innate *rapprochement* between men and who develop, so as not to disappoint their followers, the illusion of the eternal preservation of matter in a form recognised and loved - hence the myth of eternal paradise where the dead are supposed to all meet up again in their living form. And on the other we have some Eastern religions which accept the fickleness of the world and even envisage an eternal return in a perfect form."

"And what is unique to this new interpretation of the cosmos on Earth using Complementarity, is that it finds a common accord between these two visions of humanity in agreement. It's great!"

"By recognising that altruism, in other words love, is a founding value in our societies, and by revealing the evident reality of the renewal of the single Consciousness in every conscious mind from generation to generation, when displayed in human relations Complementarity eliminates the incompatibility of beliefs. Religion can rediscover its etymological meaning for all individuals linked together through new technology."

"But for that to happen, this new panel of illusion needs to be accepted by as many people as possible doesn't it?"

"A better idea would be to present things differently. If we want to adjust the illusions that pepper our existence on Earth in line with the latest scientific discoveries, it is time to light up our lives with a real generator of shared happiness. And Complementarity offers the possibility of such joy.

RENEWING HEAVEN ON EARTH

"So it's by controlling the dispersion of fragments of the unique Consciousness that we will find peace. That should be done partly through containing the exponential expansion of the global population and partly by uniting the various fragments through shared interest groups."

"And in order to contain the population explosion, we need to encourage the elderly to commit Orthothanasia, and thus enable their fragment of the total Consciousness that they provided a temporary home for to rejoin the whole before being shared out again among very young minds."

"And to create the shared interest groups, in order that a number of minds should come together, we need to ensure communication continues to develop. Obviously the Internet is the shining example of this wonderful momentum which pushes us to link our senses"

"And thus people will be able to be individuals within a fraternal group – human Complementarity."

"It's perfect."

"Then why, at this precise moment, are you doubting you new venture will succeed? You should have confidence in your reasoning; it stands up and you know it does. So why, when everything seems to be coming together down to the smallest detail so that this dream can be a success, are you trembling with fear?"

"If this did all come into effect, what would be the next step?"

"What do you mean?"

"I think humanity is calmly moving towards something revolutionary, something to replace this society which is careening towards ruin. Making everything profit-based is doomed to failure because within each and every one of us there is a shared heritage that has nothing to do with money."

"A society that has managed to even make bringing people together profit-based will burn itself out."

"That's where Complementarity's strength lies; promoting this bond that leads us all to work together to the best of our intelligence, making Complementarity the engine of a new society…"

"So we need to rethink our society in these terms and separate the effects of Consciousnesses in action from a profit-based mentality. Money needs to be defined as it used to be – a method of sharing skills. We need to reaffirm the founding role of the community, or people coming together. We need to build a future using the momentum of Complementarity."

"And enable the elderly to liberate the fragment of Consciousness that they have been harbouring in their mortal coil – a coil which is now showing signs of effective decay – so that the fragment can rejoin the total Consciousness before doubtless being renewed in brand new minds."

"If everyone manages to individualise themselves within the comforting framework of human society, and if they live to the full so as to feed the World of Ideas with new feelings, then the absolute divinity of the imperial mechanism could be renewed on Earth."

"With the development of the Internet and other communication systems enabling people to join together in the privacy of their cognition, with digital progress meaning we can gradually memorise the occurrences of our senses, then Complementarity becomes possible in these calm times."

"Do you really think we are living in calm times?"

"What mankind is violently confronted with is the insidious perversion of the definition of financial power as well as the naive and secular attempts to explain the cosmos in a fantasy way that is unfortunately etched in marble."

"But those who inspired the writers were visited by angels too."

"They were in another time. And the revelations made to them only had a sense in the context of the era. In fact, they should never have been written down for all eternity. You should always await the return of divine inspiration."

"No, the real cause of the problem is that different interpretations of the same message were allowed to develop."

"Undoubtedly. So you think it's all a matter of interpretation?"

"There's also the progress of mankind which has shone a different light on reality."

"You mean digitisation?"

"It's clear that without the possibility of handling data in such a simplified way, we would never have been able to elaborate such a system as Complementarity – it goes with the times."

"It took a visit from an angel today and a simple maxim whispered in a deafening half-light for you to feel a need to calmly express the results of your thinking."

"You helped me too."

"That's what I just said."

"But aside from a simple exercise in deduction, we have honed a perfectly viable system which is also a system in harmony with the entirety of even the most advanced scientific discoveries as well as the innermost impulses of the human being."

"That's a little pretentious isn't it?"

"It's true. But Complementarity could wittingly become something of a reformed moral."

"Again!"

"I so wanted to understand the private functioning of the being, but failing that, laying the foundations for a new way of living is as important isn't it?"

"There is in this human capacity for turning the fruits of the imagination into reality, and therefore for taking an impromptu trip in the World of Ideas, the proof of the human's demi-god status. All humans are brilliant in every way. And if some manage to concentrate this ethereal genius, it is just one talent more, lent by history. What is clear is that the enterprising nature of nervous systems in action, which share, more than an approximate appearance, the very essence of their definition."

"More than brothers, these complementary individuals work together to create a Heaven on Earth, a tight community in which everyone can be themselves in an effective Complementarity..."

THE CONSCIENCE OF HUMANITY

"And even if we have to start with political unity, the ideal of serenity will be achieved once the uniqueness of the Consciousness on Earth, the Consciousness of humanity, is recognised."

"I have two comments to make. Firstly, I don't understand what you mean by the ideal of serenity. Did we not work out earlier that the point of life on Earth arose in part from the tensions and struggles which favour the participation of all in the construction of the future? Yet serenity implies a sort of inaction doesn't it?"

"The ideal of all policy, as we saw earlier, is to promote individualisation within a united or fraternal group. And you can't have fraternity without opposition and in-fighting. But the group reforms each time its integrity comes under threat. The serenity I'm talking about is to be found at this level. The internal struggles are there to develop the point of the game by encouraging creative strategies. But the foundations of a united group are reinforced by a reassuring serenity."

"OK, I get the serenity part. But don't your worry that once the unique Consciousness is recognised, there will be no place left – or at least not such a prestigious place – for Consciousnesses that express themselves through personalities?"

"These billions of Consciousnesses, we have recognised them all as being scattered fragments of a shattered unique Consciousness. However, rebuilding the broken links through the intermediary of the Internet and communication will restore the original network, as in a healthy organism. Also, people in Complementarity will work to ensure the continuation of this healed organism, humanity. And individualities will continue to express themselves in the interest of effectively participating in the human destiny. That's the fresh start in human relations."

"The problem I have, if we look at the united nature of a humanity that thinks and acts as a closed organism, is that in comparing it to nervous systems which act on a totally different scale, individuals are by analogy cells of this organism. Yet when a cell in the body of a human or an animal asserts its individuality over others, it can look like a cancer. And it always ends up by being harmful to the organism it is part of."

"But that's forgetting the basic particularity of the human exception I believe."

"You mean that man has a completely different relationship with the organism he is part of than the cell does with the body?"

"I do think the fact we have a fragment from another dimension deep within us._This extract of Consciousness which is the cornerstone of our very definition, leads man to develop a transcendency regarding humanity that does not exist in a cell's relations within an active nervous system."

"And it's this transcendence, arising from the sharing of the unique Consciousness within him_that gives man his instinct to discover, to understand and to transform his life. These extracts of divinity, which once reunited will give this common origin the power to act, are the fossil imprint of their god."

"So there is nothing to fear from someone with an extremely strong personality. Everyone will eventually recognise their Complementarity and work together to give humanity a future."

"Especially since the happiness felt by someone when they manage to make their mark in a beneficial way is automatically balanced on a global scale so that the movement working away deep down is nothing but a pleasurable thrill."

"A sort of agitation that favours creativity?"

"That's exactly it!"

"So it's necessary for people to affirm themselves. Everyone needs their involvement in the construction of a glorious future to be recognised. But everyone needs this recognition by their peers for an existence which, for want of openly influencing the passage of time, will be able to offer humanity, through the act of Orthothanasia, all the riches of their recorded feelings via the fabulous World of Ideas."

"Yes! That is how the role of each and every one in the construction of Heaven on Earth is finally recognised."

DIRECTED CATHARSIS

"I'm finding it difficult to express myself now."

"What's going on?"

"Have you heard of the opaque box experiment?"

"I don't think so. What is it?"

"They gave an opaque box to a boy. They told him there was a sweet inside. To get it out he had to do the following: first he had to insert a wand into a hole in the top of the box, tap three times and then turn it anti-clockwise. Then he would be able to open a little drawer on the side of the box and get to the sweet. The little boy tried. He inserted the wand in the hole, tapped three times, turned the wand anti-clockwise, opened the drawer, found the sweet inside and was delighted to have done so."

"He got the hang of it quickly."

"Yes he did. Then they tried the same experiment with a chimpanzee. They taught him the same method and he mastered it and recovered his prize which was a piece of banana."

"So far there seems no difference between a child's reasoning and that of a primate."

"Indeed, both learned a *modus operandi* without a real link with the desired goal. Both managed to achieve the goal. But everything changed in the second phase of the experiment."

"I'm listening."

"Well, the second time, instead of giving them a totally opaque box, they gave them a transparent one and it was quite plain the drawer containing the prize was in no way blocked by any kind of complex mechanism – nothing to stop it simply being opened straight away."

"So it was possible just to go straight to the prize?"

"Exactly, and that is what the chimpanzee did. After a quick examination of the inside of the box, he disregarded the method he had been taught and simply opened the drawer and got his prize."

"But the little boy didn't?"

"No. Undoubtedly the little boy understood how the box worked and that the drawer was independent of the hole on the top but he repeated the exact same method he had been taught."

"A method that appeared to be unnecessary to obtain his prize."

"But a method he had been taught by his kind, by his peers and so it therefore takes on a transcendental importance. These actions, stripped of any kind of usefulness to achieve a real goal become vital in order to exist in this entity which contains him: humanity. The ritual had become a crucial part of the recognition of his membership of the group. The chimp couldn't care less. He does not have a jewel inside him, a fragment of the total Consciousness, a sliver of the absolute."

"What's so traumatic about this experiment for you?"

"Well, the power of the conscious human being, his aptitude for perfectibility and over-humanisation, is derives from his capacity to build transcendence. In accepting and performing rituals and other traditions, man integrates himself in a history that is his own. And so he evolves, and so he perfects himself."

"And you're worried that your doubts and questioning put you on a level with a primate rather than a conscious human?"

"And yet that's what brought an angel to cross my path – this time spent questioning the basis of rites and traditions inherited from another age has enabled me to pare down the empirical religions."

"What do you mean?"

"The retrospective interpretation of words left on paper by the torrent of ideas that made up a predominantly oral tradition has only betrayed the truth. Because the message has always been the same: 'There is only one Consciousness, only one.' I had to reject all the gold-leafed superfluity in order for the message to be told to me. So I acted like a primate for the good cause. And that, in itself, is something."

A SCATTERED UNITY

"The link which unites us is too strong for a little fraternal debate to fracture. But better still; the question of individual responsibility can be put into perspective with the new accessories of Complementarity."

"What type of responsibility?"

"The responsibility to do with actions which imply a categorical reorientation of the future of several people. Courts charged with judging brutal acts would no longer be able to punish a man but just control the ripple effect by preventing recidivism among others."

"I don't understand."

"And yet it's simple. By accepting the definition of human ambition as ultimately to create Heaven on Earth for all, and by recognising the complementary form this ambition must take in each of us, it is right to assume collective responsibility for all that happens on Earth. And if that's the case it is difficult to pass judgement on others."

"You're going too far. You mean to say that individuals are striving towards the same goal and therefore the entirety of what happens is necessary and essential in reaching it?"

"From the moment something happens, there is every reason to believe it will contribute to the creation of a wonderful future."

"But in that case, the courts and their sentences are also necessary and essential!"

"We have to stop reproaching others for what in any case could only have occurred in that way. We just need to condemn as an example. And by example I mean effective communication of judgement. The player who has messed up the start of the game and who doesn't manage to find his place in the structure so as to be able to offer the community the product of his individuality at work can decide to start anew. Just like through Orthothanasia, it is conceivable that an honourable exit could be offered to those who seem to have made a mistake in their ambition."

"You're thinking of the death penalty?"

"I think the convicted person should be given the choice as an example of continuing this life or moving on to the next."

"But that's already the case. Some people commit suicide in prison. This would simply be recognising the validity of such a choice."

"Above all, it would have the advantage of giving greater value to a life spared. By opting to prolong their life, a convicted person would commit themselves to taking advantage of all remaining possibilities to make the best of things."

"Yet another type of catharsis."

"That's right. By setting known limits to the temporal aspect of his existence, the conscious human – the would-be superman, enables his will to focus on its momentum within a reasonable time lapse. That way he rids his history of all excesses that encumber his spirit."

"And the convicted man has an immediate need for catharsis?"

"Not him in particular! I don't know why I'm talking to you about this now. No doubt to justify a measure which could seem anachronistic – the return of the death penalty. Along with Orthothanasia, we're describing a bit of a macabre ethic aren't we?"

"It's primarily an ethic which reconciles man with his own death isn't it? Official religions, despite their propensity to create wonderful myths intended to offer the living the illusion of a historic continuity after death, have failed to do that. Complementarity offers a real geometry, based on an obvious fact!"

"Or what you believe to be one…"

"In any case, everything will disappear in the end – mankind and its culture."

"Why?"

"Because everything changes. Nothing is stable and destined to continue in some kind of illusory eternity."

"Because you think even eternity is bound to disappear? The problem you are throwing up is fundamentally a human one. What I mean is, it's already written in the historic experience of reality. But if you eliminate time too, if you visualise all generations following one after the other, you will notice the fundamental point of this reality of fables."

"On the contrary, it's you who foresees the end of everything in the passing of time! So don't accuse me of being too human. I'm like you – condemned to submit to time which passes. And I would have difficulty stepping out of that to visualise time geometrically as you suggest."

"To do that you would have to recall the hypothesis we started with."

"You don't attach much importance to the fantastical circumstances which implanted this "hypothesis" as you call it in your untamed spirit."

"This revelation if you prefer."

"What I think is..."

"Listen. In recognising the unique and whole nature of the Consciousness, shattered and dispersed among all those who deserve it, we can detach it from time and put it under the microscope."

"Agreed. But what do you expect to find in this conscientious dissection?"

"I just want you to see that if you separate it from history, the Consciousness sweeps aside all sensitivity. In other words, sensitivity – and above all responsibility – in each of us is found in historical events, at least for the most part. And using the intermediary of the World of Ideas, the most talented having access."

"So what you are trying to make me understand is that we're all responsible for past history?"

"Exactly."

"That's appalling."

"On the contrary, it multiplies our possibilities tenfold. In admitting that conflicts were the representation of an internal shock of creative forces of the total Consciousness, then we remove the seriousness that can pull at a student's heart strings."

"Then history becomes the story of a great game..."

"And the men living it are selfless players in an obsessive but sublime masquerade. I'm for breaking it all up! That's how we will free these players, these people, from the weight of history. Who cares about a 'duty to remember'? In any case, we're all guilty of endless agitation on this little blue planet."

"You've got it."

INNOCENCE FOUND

"Freed from the reproaches that we used to be subject to, freed from the remorse that could eat away at an active nervous system, home for a few billion seconds to a divine fragment, we can now act in Complementarity with others like us to set up a carbon copy of Heaven on Earth."

"You have finally discovered the meaning of life!"

"It's true. I am hungry to do something once again because I know what direction the immeasurable effects of my will will take. I have understood the hidden meaning of all this incredible technology: to link human Consciousnesses together to recreate on Earth the whole and unique Consciousness – God."

"And the memorising of senses which the exponential increase in digital memory capacity has now made possible enables its contents to be shared between all. You no longer need to train your mind to prise open the heavy doors of the World of Ideas to find inspiration. From now on, everyone can seek sensorial sustenance there."

"That's absolutely right! Consciousnesses linked together with those who have access to all of humanity's memory, will join forces to give all men the power to live in Complementarity."

"That's great!"

"But first of all, we have to reconcile human beings with death. It should no longer be considered as a retreat from Earthly life. We have to stop telling these stories that are supposed to give hope of a well-earned rest for mankind after their short passage on Earth. We have to concentrate on the essential: the unique nature of the Consciousness which implies an absolute bond between human beings and planet Earth."

"A perpetual reincarnation?"

"An equitable distribution among all young minds that deserve, for better and for worse, that we contain the demographic explosion which is constantly reducing the size of the fragments of Consciousness."

"And to achieve that, in order to normalise this human population, we have to suggest, and explain, that the elderly should free their Consciousness so that it can be mixed in with others to finally enter a brand new mind. This fragment, with all the innocence offered by continual incarnation, can live again by amassing more feelings and experiences to be bequeathed to humanity once its destiny is achieved."

"It seems perfect."

"It is."

"It's now clear that this new system, which aims to reform tradition to improve our life conditions, presents reality in a light that puts it in contradiction with those same traditions."

"But it's for the general good."

"It doesn't matter. People will do everything they can to preserve that which, taught to them since the beginning of their humanisation, continues to guide them through this gigantic metaphysical void which contains us all."

"So what's your idea?"

"We have to speak to the young, those who, discovering tradition's fingerprints on reality, allow themselves to doubt."

"The Internet is there to make the job easier. The digital memory of humanity is only in its infancy but it's already a giant step."

"Especially since they can now bounce their ideas off their 'planet-mates'!"

"Yes, that's a bit of luck."

"We have to grab this opportunity to put forward a new idea. It creates scope for strengthening the bonds between us – more than brothers, complementary individuals. And if everyone finds their ideal place in this functional puzzle of human activity, and defends it and uses it to multiply the efforts of their own individuality, then the progression of all humanity towards a balanced and healthy destiny will also be multiplied."

"And people will be happier?"

"Instances of happiness and unhappiness are shared out in equal measure among humanity. It wouldn't be a good idea to tamper with this balance but the strength of such a system would lead you to think so."

"In theory, there's no fundamental difference between the current level of happiness and that which would exist if you accept the precepts of Complementarity. So then why would people sign up for it? They believe they have found meaning in the religion they currently follow. They don't need anything more to live a happy life."

"But take a look at the young, those who already have a natural access to the enormous bank of online data. Some of them are questioning the validity in this day and age of texts written thousands of years ago."

"But you already admitted, those texts were inspired by the same divine source. And it's this same inexhaustible source that gave you your initial inspiration for this entire wonderful craziness."

"Precisely. Starting from a similar awakening, it is time to reconsider the consequences and make deductions from them. The purity of the initial revelation is well and truly there. It is up to us to develop the meaning as we have been doing. Now is the time to assume the essence by updating the implications of this routine in our lives."

"If I've understood you correctly, your aim is to model the new rules of life by returning to the first obvious fact revealed."

"That's what we've been doing isn't it?"

"Evidently we have removed the shoddy ornaments of simple and trivial concepts that come to mind when you give yourself the time to think about them. The *rapprochement* between humans, the competition which is created and which divides them for a time, the excessive growth in their number which brings nothing more than a vague feeling of a lessening of one's impact on the world – these are a few snippets of evident concepts which currently constrain us."

"And the law of Complementarity which ought to govern human relations…"

"Mankind has already abused it but unknowingly. At least it has the advantage of revealing to us honestly one of the intrinsic dynamics that drives us all. What we need now is for this law to help us define political objectives don't we?"

"It would be a proof of integrity!"

"Complementarity must help design the momentum that will generate a future which obviously should be sublime. Because the initial naivety that young people are attributed upon their return to life is a chance that we should try to nurture in order to be happy. Excess of conscience harms happiness in this cosmos void of meaning."

REPARING THE SPHERE

"I want to talk to you about love – the love that makes you forget everything and concentrate on a bond you wish indestructible."

"When two beings meet and everything makes sense."

"That's it. I have already met people who seem to match perfectly the indented shape of my Consciousness. They are sufficiently rare in number for me to remember every detail of these encounters."

"And you let them get away?"

"I couldn't hold on to them. They let themselves get sucked up by the whirlwinds around us. But I did end up sure of one thing – I knew their Consciousnesses."

"We already spoke of that. Your two Consciousnesses doubtless inhabited the same person in a previous generation. They were divided when that person died and then were shared between your two minds in your youth. And when your two bodies met, your Consciousnesses recognised each other."

"It's not that simple. Consciousnesses cannot be compared to cells which undergo mitosis by dividing and becoming two identical cells to fill the growing number of new minds. On the contrary, the unique Consciousness seems roughly to divide up without waiting to preserve the pre-established mixture!"

"So love-at-first-sight would be the meeting of 'lumps' of Consciousness which remained intact from the initial flow. And the feeling of love which grew stronger day after day would be the confirmation of a slow recognition in the other Consciousness of a scattered fragment of a past liaison?"

"As a concept it's quite nice!"

"I think love is rather the proof of a shared unique Consciousness. And to make a commitment, it draws on signs coming from education and context. But in theory we are all capable of becoming attached to anyone. Because we all harbour Consciousnesses which fit together perfectly."

"So if only we made time to take an interest in them, we could fall in love with everyone on Earth."

"Indeed, from the moment we focalise all our Consciousness on someone, it is impossible for us to feel anything other than love or hate for them – in other words some kind of interest or empathy. Because we will eventually find a piece of Complementarity in the other."

"And it's on this feeling that we have to hang all the policies seeking to govern human relations."

"That's what happens now isn't it?"

"This feeling shared by all human beings is a major part of their humanity. Even more than that, it reveals the reality of their definition; an individualised mortal coil enclosing within it a fragment of their divinity."

"Isn't that a new illusion?"

"Contradict me – I expected nothing more. Try to knock it down with recognisable facts. I can't."

"Animals as far from man as possible are also capable of love. Isn't that proof that love is nothing to do with the human Consciousness?"

"Animals know this feeling for one reason only: to ensure the future of their species. Man can love without seeking to procreate. He has managed to detach this natural impulse from its primary purpose. What's more, I am sure that the Consciousness stretches far further than the neural bodies of the human species."

"What do you mean?"

"I am deeply convinced that this unique Consciousness crosses space and time and touches everything that is. Its fragments are well-reasoned and incorporated into a mind because the particular support that is the human body permits it. But it is parallel to the fact of existing."

"You mean that everything that exists in the cosmos prints an inflexion on the total Consciousness?"

"I couldn't have put it better."

"On their death, the individual frees the fragment of this unique Consciousness that they have been harbouring for a limited time, enabling it to rejoin the total. It then shares its history with the total memory and, after having been combined with its kind; its essence is shared out again among young minds."

"A sequence which enables it to contemplate the Being in its entirety, detached from time and three dimensions."

"It's a lovely picture isn't it?"

"A lovely picture which has the advantage of being in harmony with the current state of knowledge."

"If you like."

A PRIVILEGED PLACE

"What significance is there in a terrestrial event compared to the immeasurable immensity of the universe?"

"The significance is given by the mind that takes an interest in it. And viewed like this, there is no doubt the Earth is very definitely the centre of the universe. Until proof to the contrary, who would argue with me on that?"

"You're ignoring celestial movements which create elliptical rotations, the centre of which is anything but a planet."

"No. I simply look up to the sky and I notice that everything is turning around my observation point."

"Yes but the latest technologies have enabled us to move this observation point huge distances from us."

"But the image always comes back to us. We are irrefutably linked to our environment. And if one day we leave this cradle of humanity and spread out through the cosmos, fluid communication will then become impossible. Therefore we will have lost the possibility of linking our Consciousnesses together to rebuild our divinity."

"What do you mean?"

"God is the sum of all Consciousnesses effectively in action. It is up to us to enable his emergence in the midst of all this chaos by linking the fragments together to recreate the original state of our unique Consciousness. We are close to achieving our goal. Afterwards it will become impossible. It'll be way too late."

"Should we be satisfied with this unavoidable *rapprochement* amongst those who oppose adventurous spirits?"

"That's the power of humanity. Once the demographic explosion has been tamed, a humanity made up of young people avid for knowledge, would be able to find spiritual fulfilment on a planet of the right size. People will be able to act in Complementarity for personal fulfilment for the entire species."

"It's Heaven on Earth!"

"You know what?"

"Tell me."

"When you became convinced of this this morning…"

"When the angel came to speak to me?"

"If you like. It offered you the key to a marvellous way of organising humanity. There is food for thought there for its very future. Today's society, in which a slave mentality

163

has taken over and everything has a price tag, thus creating a scale of totally abstract values, is certainly not one that will allow humanity to flourish peacefully. We have to get back to basics. The *rapprochement* between people is key. And if death is seen as a liberation for an eternal return, then humanity will become younger. And this naive army will largely be able to live again because that is its destiny - once people have understood that happiness lies not in possessions but in the *rapprochement* which inevitably draws us to each other, to connect the senses, to connect with each other's Consciousnesses, to repair the original explosion, the debris of which is now shared between an exponential number of new minds awaiting a Consciousness. The new means of communication are the key. They will enable us to copy the uniqueness of the Consciousness in connecting our senses."

"You have said it all! That gives a meaning to life doesn't it?"

"Yes. By detaching ourselves from an overly materialistic culture and moving to the eternal non-materialness of virtual reality, all is squared. That will mean we have already succeeded in producing a fair copy of the inner workings of the World of Ideas. And inspiration will become easier, more accessible, more widespread, leading to the emergence of a young and artistic humanity, the coming supermen."

"Don't hurry things! You have skipped a few generations. Before we see the next stage of evolution, humanity will first have to learn to persevere within their being and that goes hand-in-hand with the preservation of the entire biosphere on Earth."

"But isn't mankind supposed to one day leave Earth to discover new inhabitable planets and thus spread out through the cosmos?"

"I already told you, I'm afraid that once separated by a distance that makes fluid communication a physical impossibility, the divine part in each of us will change and regress. But I say that based on current scientific knowledge. Quantum physics doesn't appear to have been sufficiently incorporated into communication technology as yet."

"But what is true is that if the Complementarity described here is understood by many and incorporated into their life ethics, then community life here on planet Earth will once again be interesting enough and valued enough to be lived intensely."

"Because you don't think that's the case any more today?"

"I believe I have better things to do on Earth than consume."

"Isn't that what you're doing? I mean, if business wasn't doing so well, would you have been able to push yourself to think about all this? Think about it because you're a little quick to mock this relatively comfortable society which offers you time and the material means for whatever you think worth it."

"You're no doubt right. But I worry about those who only find happiness in the frenetic consumption of goods that are all perishable in the end. They aren't doing anything for themselves or humanity. They live useless lives don't they?"

"Of course not! They all experience intense moments in their well-organised lives. And by sharing their existence with others, they too take part in copying the World of Ideas on Earth. They are part of the humanity that gathers in the Consciousness. The distinctive feature of every existence is the very basis of Complementarity. They are perfectly complementary to each other!"

"But in that case everyone can find a particular place that renders them complementary to the rest of humanity."

"And if he shares his emotions, the sum of his feelings, with the global community on Earth, he will automatically be incorporated in the constituent momentum for the copying on Earth of the absolute truth. He will take part in the creation of an imitation divinity."

"That's cool."

TRAUMATISED TRANSCENDENCE

"The human exception is transcendence. It is the firm belief in the hidden sense. We need to bring back this traumatised transcendence in the convincing hope of Complementarity!"

"Are you implying modern life has corrupted this access to transcendence which remains the distinctive feature of mankind?"

"It has put it on the back-burner of the things a modern individual worries about. And I'm not even talking about religions. Who can claim to have access to a clear and simple presentation of reality? And yet this sober elegance exists. The disjointed construction of the material world has made us forget that behind all this exists a really simple idea."

"I'm listening."

"Have you heard of automatic writing?"

"Yes, and I've often done it. In poetry for example, it enables you to discover really amazing new concepts."

"Where do you think it comes from?"

"We've already talked about this. It's a simple way of connecting to the World of Ideas."

"Isn't it chance rather that enables you to form associations between amazing ideas?"

"Chance is just a justification people use when they don't know the real causes – or when those causes are so numerous or on such a large scale it is impossible to list them all."

"So chance doesn't really exist – it's simply a jumble of cause and effect."

"Where are you going with this?"

"Do you think time ticks by in the same way millions of light years from Earth?"

"I've never thought about it."

"I think the difficulty with our perception of the world resides in our scientific method which is based on the hypothetico-deductive. We need to distance ourselves from this to understand, to find inspiration directly in the perfect World of Ideas that inspires artists. But the result will doubtless be a total and simple understanding of the Being with an inability to transcribe it in accessible language. So to try to put across the beauty, we make the message more and more complex until it is completely obscure - as if we wanted to preserve the structure from any chance interpretation. We create new concepts and we preserve the essential."

"That's what you're trying to do isn't it?"

"Of course."

"You yourself are afraid of the validity of your ideas aren't you?"

"It's not that I'm afraid. As conclusive and deep as this discussion is, it has opened a chasm at my feet and I'm hesitant about jumping in, that's all."

"And yet we both agreed it's the solution to many problems so why wait any longer?"

"I guess it's just that up until now humanity has progressed without really having need of a leader."

"And the numerous prophets who were contacted by the same angel as you, and who interpreted his words as they could based on their culture and their science; they all pushed for humanity's creative expression."

"You take me for one of them? That's a laugh."

"And the angel who chose you to spread this great idea – are you now denying him?"

"But what angel? My vision was blurred. My consciousness was altered. I weakened and possibly dreamed. Do you really believe that in the 21st century angels still appear to the enlightened? You'd better get real. I have a fertile imagination and I'm also full enough of myself that sometimes I feel like taking an illusion for reality."

"I don't believe you now. You seemed in such turmoil when you grabbed my arm. I'm sure you saw something. And this diaphanous cloud gave you a wonderful present, a crucial revelation capable of enlightening the Consciousness of humanity. It's natural to be afraid – you weren't prepared for this. Who could be? But your role as a messenger began today. You shared with me the message. I listened to you and I understood."

"And you're still in turmoil aren't you?"

"Perhaps what you need is solid access to transcendence. You're too much of a loner for that. The Complementarity you talk about with such passion needs to feel and understand the inner *rapprochement* that stimulates the yearning between people. How can you be satisfied with your reclusive life? If you want to even dip your toe in the reality you are proposing, you will have to learn to live in the human community. Absolute transcendence is to be found in the inquisitive regard of the other."

"But you share your emotions with others. And you live with me. Together we can win over the Consciousnesses scattered through the labyrinth of existence. We need to dare to share all this. Together we are strong. We're facing a huge obstacle but we can overcome it together."

"What obstacle? What are you talking about?"

"When you open your eyes in the morning, what spurs you to go to the effort of getting out of bed?"

"I suppose just habit to a certain extent. I have to go and live my day, the work, the leisure and all those perfectly unnecessary moments."

"Don't you have a goal?"

"You mean I have doubtless found one and you are doubtless right. I'm excited about this new direction my life is going to take. I've been freed from the prison of consumerism. I'm going to share the revelation and what a revelation it is!"

"So you're now the carrier of an important message. You'll have to put your back into it."

"So this is my new transcendence, a few simple words linking me to the cosmos. My life has taken a very interesting turn. I thought myself a stranger to this planet dotted with inert Consciousnesses. Now I am an actor, complementary to the others. And the Consciousnesses are striving for *rapprochement* and symbiosis with a view to recreating that which has been destroyed: the unique Consciousness."

"You're getting carried away! That's good."

"I'm beginning to understand the reason for all this. I'm beginning to understand what happened that brought us to this point. People have lived for too long in illusions created by others smarter than themselves. They have long believed in a truth that is now laughable. And all because they had a chasm at their feet, a monstrous void of meaning, the visible result of the feel-good factor being ripped out of them. We had to wait until man had tamed matter in order to create the means of sticking the pieces back together."

"Internet is a chance."

"Communication networks that are ever faster and more personal have contributed to the emergence of this reality. People want to communicate with each other because they need to feel they are on the same wave length. The innate attraction between people turns out to be fundamental to their existence. The need to communicate is the basis of the anthropological definition."

"And love too."

"But love has been recognised as an essential human condition for millennia. What's new in the 21st century is the exponential development of the means that enable an individual to be on the same wave length as thousands, if not millions, of others."

"The communication boom has made a planetary empathy possible now. Just as a crowd of people united by a shared feeling acts in an autonomous and original way, minds linked together through senses and cognition enable a meta- consciousness to appear. And these Consciousnesses brought together though the experience of virtual compassion give rise to a copy of the unique Consciousness, a Consciousness proven to be almost divine."

"But how can this Consciousness express itself and act if it is not mediated by a mind directly linked to a nervous system capable of acting on its environment?"

"On the contrary, this unique Consciousness is made up of a delicate assembly of individual Consciousnesses scattered among all minds, all active nervous systems, linked together in this tangle of identical stimuli and shared emotions. It is connected humanity that can act and react to the fluctuation of ideas from this single entity."

"It's instant universal democracy!"

"Better than that because in this statistical representation of humanity's aspirations, there are no leaders and no elections. People interact between themselves in a natural and spontaneous way. There is no need for coercion because the emerging ideas are incorporated and treated by the exertion of virtual sharing."

"There's a new form of transcendence! And thus this human faculty also finds itself interlocking in the organised meanderings of the binary system. After the *rapprochement* of the senses and the collective memory, this is the third founding element of the definition of man to materialise on Earth through creative humanity."

"It is now recognised that everyone on Earth has a shared plan. They aim together to design an environment similar to the system that animates their being beyond their existence on Earth."

"They desperately seek to work in Complementarity to achieve this, under the direct control of the founding organisation which governs their definition of man beyond their corporal existence on Earth."

"Oh come on…"

"It's clear isn't it?"

"I suppose what you call 'their definition of man beyond their existence on Earth' is just the divine part in man. That is what we have so far called the 'Consciousness', all instances of which, present in each human mind, are the scattered fragments of one single entity, the god of men. As for the 'founding organisation', it is in part this primordial uniqueness and in part the connectivity which exists between all instances of Consciousness detached from time. In other words, the universal memory of feelings and ideas. Over the generations, this vast data bank which everyone feeds with their own experiences, contributes to the inspiration of new humans so that they can achieve their goal."

"That being the creation on Earth of all that!"

"Exactly. Through the huge development of memorisation and communication technology, humanity is seeking to recreate with its own hands, the wonderful components of its own definition in the cosmos here on Earth."

"Man seeks to consciously control his transcendence."

THE MAN IN HUMANITY

"At the dawn of the 21st century, multiple technological advances have managed to make concrete, in the daily reality of humanity, the objective purpose of human existence."

"Shared, communicated and memorised, to engender a creative and generous global Consciousness."

"But in concrete terms, how should someone live in order to consciously take part in this wonderful scheme?"

"We are all heirs to a genetic heritage which lends us certain skills and a few innate aptitudes, and we are fired by a fragment of the total Consciousness which links all active Consciousnesses to the universal memory as long as we can find the path which gives us access to it. So we need to make the best use of our abilities and live our lives to the full. The quantity and quality of new sensations recorded by an active nervous system will be what humanity will thank it for."

"So we have to do as much as possible with what we start out with."

"We have to be the artist of our own lives."

"So it is better to reject the miniscule variations in mood of monastic inaction for a life full of ups and downs packed with emotions and feelings."

"It would be better for the person and for all of humanity, yes."

"The person couldn't be criticised in any way…"

"We've now accepted that there is an equal share of sorrow and of joy. Someone who experiences intense happiness will also suffer periods of deep despair. But he will live his life as a human on Earth to the full."

"He will live his feelings unreservedly, whether they be love or hate. In any case, these two accesses to mental plenitude which reveal all the interest shown in someone, will accompany him throughout his life in the human community."

"That is how followers of Complementarity should live their lives: concerned with offering humanity the quintessence of the achievements of a life with a starting stock being that which his genetic heritage has bequeathed him and the dexterity of access to the marvellous interconnectivity of Consciousnesses and their memories. As a bonus, he has the possibility of being inhabited by a fragment of the total which has passed intact through the mixing process and so will generate the apparition of supernatural pre-dispositions for the qualities of a prior – now deceased – host."

"He will have to live in Complementarity with his kind for his existence to have meaning in all this chaos. By dedicating his actions to the unity of Consciousnesses, he will manage to complete the table of honours awarded to the most alive among them. Then finally the moment of retirement will arrive, a complete retirement so that he can liberate this blue fragment which has been with him all these years."

"Once his work is done, his load of emotions ready to rejoin the universal memory of feelings and ideas, he will choose, fully aware of the work he has carried out, to commit Orthothanasia and to leave his terrestrial incarnation for a while."

"And avoid the predictable decline of his flesh…"

"And avoid offering innocent young people the risible image of the inevitable and welcome decline, which reminds us all that nothing is permanent."

GOD IS ALIVE

"We have found God scattered in all the effective Consciousnesses in action. He thinks in the minds of men and acts through their arms. He doesn't need a home away from Earth. He is right here with us."

"And we have found a way to make him visible to our eyes, by building a copy of the divine Consciousness with our own hands…"

"Where we seek to renew the timeless memory of humanity."

"That is for those who want to believe, who have been brought up with this irreparable need for his comforting presence. And what about for the others, those for whom life is nothing but an infernal curse which reincarnates Consciousnesses in pain and fear?"

"For them, this god is simply a useful but illusory mental construction that has no reality other than the words that describe him. What's important is the recognition that life continues here on Earth after death. Even if the beings are only rarely recognisable, the illusion is manifestly real here."

"And the definitive result of the complementary work of all mankind, that towards which each process engendered by the will to act of all human beings must definitively lean, is the creation on Earth of an Eden-like environment, perfect for a sufficient number of minds in action."

"By 'sufficient' you mean all connected?"

"Sharing all their ideas and the images of their senses in a recognised plan to found a perfect new democracy. In other words one without real leaders, but stirred up by tensions that generate intense creativity. Together, arguing and making up like brothers depending on the context, these people will see appearing on the virtual horizon, an active Consciousness that distributes ideas that will have the shape, the wisdom and the bounty of their illusory gods."

"That gives hope."

"It's the least we can do."

MISSION ACCOMPLISHED

"So is that it then? You have completed your quest. You have found both a meaning for life on Earth as well as the outline of the divinity that everyone apparently already knew but who you wanted to ignore as a challenge."

"It's true. I'm not unhappy with myself. By revealing the true aim of human work I have found serenity. In contemplating its work in creation, I cannot but understand its dedication to the hard work of an entire life. And I have found my place in this prestigious enterprise that man has got it into his head to undertake."

"It's just most of them are unaware of it. It would be a good idea to let them know. It's likely that once informed, their efforts will increase tenfold. Their hearts will be set on playing a full part in such a wonderful adventure."

"And they'll do so with joy in their hearts at the thought of achieving such a beautiful thing!"

"I'm getting a little carried away again. Before all that we have to persuade them and my mind is becoming blurred because I can already hear the rebukes and the criticisms that will come flooding in. I'll be accused of attacking ancient structures which have supported human naivety for far too long. I'm going to have explained to me all the benefits of these illusory dogmas. And yet it is them that have brought us to our current pass."

"But if respect for human life can be put down to divine injunctions, then for a while that served the role of the human being in this variable geometric chaos of life on Earth. Now it is doing it a disservice. But how can we reconcile this nice respect and the deference for the sustainability of humanity in its current environment?"

"That's where we appeal to the optimistic realism of those who have lived beyond what they hoped for. But once again we can expect objections. Although all we're doing is speeding up their imminent rejuvenation, I risk becoming the subject of violent criticism. And yet Orthothanasia is the most beautiful way of returning a little earlier into the cycle of life for Consciousnesses trapped in a rusty old body."

"In the same way, those who have no hope of finding happiness again because they feel themselves caged in a body that no longer works properly, should be able to leave this terrestrial existence for a while, and free their impatient Consciousness to excite new minds."

"It's a choice to be made in full awareness – should everything possible be done to treat the disease or to unlock the bodily jail and free the essence? It is up to the individual and them alone to opt for the route to happiness that seems the most interesting and the most full of adventure to him."

"In the end, all this seems so obvious I find it unlikely that these innovative ideas have only grown in my brain fed on the hypothetico-deductive and automatic writing."

"You've already forgotten that it was an angel who planted the seed on the surface of your sensitivity. Without him, you wouldn't have reached this point. You would have had plenty of time to lose yourself in the olfactory labyrinth of a life devoted to pleasure. The result is there. Hundreds of pages blackened by one single mind, town between emotion and criticism. You've done well. I'm impressed."

SUSPICIOUS SIMILARITIES

"In the continuity of events that have occurred on this dusty star that is home to the very essence of our community, an element of action commands us to think."

"What remarkable thing have you found now?"

"Have you never noticed the juxtaposition of similar events that seem to be symmetrical as you get perspective?"

"You mean those apparently similar events that happen in a relatively short space of time on a human scale?"

"Would your first instinct be to assumer it's to do with an effect linking the intellectualisation of these phenomena by Consciousnesses eager for transcendence? Or, like the aftershocks of an earthquake, the propagating effect of a slight agitation in the virtual cortex of the unique Consciousness?"

"You area apparently excluding all anomalies of a metaphysical nature?"

"If you consider that the very purpose of the revelation of an angel comes in at the ground floor of a large swathe of conventional physics then yes!"

"There is enough here to incite a demonstration in isolation of this transcendence on Earth. Indeed, given the effect of natural events on the intellectual privacy of human beings, there is every reason to see here the evident proof of a total interdependence. We are tributaries of our environment in the same way that it suffers from our mood swings. In other words, in the same way as our actions interfere with the future of the biosphere, its general state affects our level of mental satisfaction, or, to put it another way, our happiness."

TRUST

"I have something I must confess."

"What is it now?"

"This wasn't the first time an angel appeared to me and revealed an important truth. It's happened at least one before."

"Go on!"

"I was still a child. I was seven, I was in the kitchen with my family at lunch time. While my mother was busy at the cooker, I was talking with my uncle. We were discussing the reasons why I had fought with my brother – two years older than me – that morning. I was defending my position as if my place among my siblings depended upon it."

"Like all siblings close in age, you were fighting for the love of your parents."

"That must be it, yes. But the most important thing is what happened next. I was completely immersed in the search for and construction of the points I wanted to make when space stopped vibrating and time stretched out to infinity. I couldn't move. Only the pupils of my eyes wondered at the situation."

"That reminds me of something."

"Exactly. The only difference between that and my experience in the underground station was that it didn't all go dark. It even got a little brighter, making everything look overexposed. I didn't see any diaphanous shape come near me, there was just a soft but sure voice that filled my ears."

"And what was the message this time?"

"Man is a robot."

"That's it?"

"Don't you get the importance of such a message in the mind of an innocent young boy? My interest in science-fiction enabled me to clothe this abstract concept in a mass of characteristics. And I understood even then that, what I would later call the 'nervous system in action' was only an intermediary for action and reaction."

"No transcendence?"

"That was to come much later. But this revelation, partial and tainted with a childlike naivety, was the starting point for a train of thought which has reached its climax today."

"You mean to say that this partial clue was given to you so as to direct your thinking for the sole purpose of preparing your mind to receive another revelation on a different scale many years later?"

"Indeed, this first indication of the nature of man on Earth enabled me to build my mental process outside of religious dogma. As no transcendence was brought to my attention, what was I to do with all these myths taught as truths by robots?"

"Carefree, liberated from the castrating incidences of influential religions, you were able to build a definition of man that was not the standard one. And the second revelation, which grew in the very depths of your neural body, has ended in you building a new ethic, freely, without reference to the empirical works of the controllers of recognised Consciousnesses."

"Complementarity is the fruit of this prolonged search. We have to believe that the time had come for a moral revelation. Or something like that."

"The only thing that is evident is that all of us human beings should work together towards a single goal: creating on Earth an environment that is like us, that is like our innermost definition. This definition makes us all complementary beings because we are all holders of a fragment of the total and unique Consciousness – which some might call a divinity. That is why we have to seek our place in society, so we can feel this Complementarity and offer our acts up to it. Environment goes hand-in-hand with the sharing of ideas and feelings, as well as their accurate memorisation so as to enable humanity to move forward, inspired by the successes and failures of the past. Inspiration enables them to accelerate the process without having to go through too many experiences which alter the trajectory."

"And above all, dying isn't a tragedy!"

"Of course not. It enables your fragment of Consciousness to link up with the whole before a new mix of it fills a young mind with its innate ability to be inspired by the gods."

"You can't help yourself from getting a little poetic can you?"

"We can't dissect such a marvellous and yet simple system without seeking to show our deep respect by giving it a little gloss…"

"That's sweet."

TITAN-ATLANTE